FINGER FOOD

An International Celebration of Bite-Sized Treats

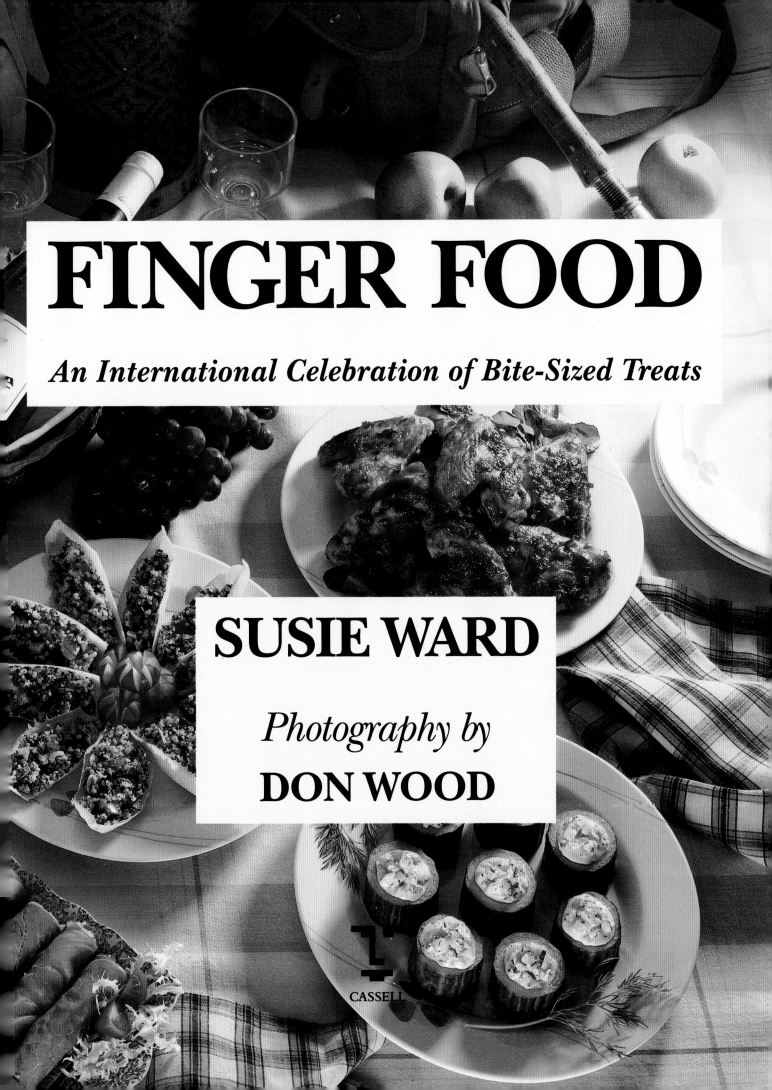

FINGER FOOD

An International Celebration of Bite-Sized Treats

SUSIE WARD

Photography by
DON WOOD

CASSELL

First published in Great Britain 1992 by
Cassell Plc
Villiers House, 41/47 Strand, London WC2N 5JE

Copyright (c) 1992 Morgan Samuel Editions
All rights reserved

British Library Cataloguing-in-Publication Data
A catalogue record for this book is available from the
British Library.

ISBN 0 304 34219 X

This book was conceived, edited, designed and produced by
Morgan Samuel Editions,
11 Uxbridge Street, London W8 7TQ.

Typesetting by Sprint Reproductions Ltd., London.
Film separations, printing and binding by
Toppan Printing Co (HK) Ltd, Hong Kong.

Contents

Introduction 6

Hosting a Finger Food Party 8

Secrets of Garnishing.............................12
  Simple Leaf and Flower Garnishes
  Fruit and Vegetable Garnishes
  More Elaborate Garnishes

Mediterranean Mezze 20
  Hummus-Filled Miniature Pittas
  Lemon-Scented Stuffed Vine Leaves
  Spinach-Phyllo Triangles
  Feta-Filled Artichoke Hearts
  Artichoke and Tomato Barquettes
  Easy Kebbeh
  Lentil and Courgette Patties
  Miniature Shish Kebabs

Russian Zakuski 26
  Stuffed Baby Beetroot
  New Potatoes with Caviar
  Finger Cabbage Rolls
  Potato Croquettes with Surprise Filling
  Marinated Mushrooms
  Curd Cheese and Ham Piroshki
  Dilled Salmon Tartlets
  Herring and Apple Rolls

A Stand-Up Supper 32
  Leek and Carrot Sticks
  Gruyère and Smoked Ham Popovers
  Individual Smoked Salmon Roulades
  Artichoke-Prawn Cups
  Steak Tartare Balls with Mustard Sauce
  Strawberry Tartlets

Spanish Tapas 36
  Costa Blanca Salad Boats
  Deep-Fried Prawns
  Vegetable Empanadas
  Lemon-Onion Sardines
  Stuffed Mussels Casino
  Sweet Peppers with Savoury Filling
  Roasted Pepper Dip
  Albondigas with Garlic Dip
  Valencian Almonds

Japanese-Style Hors d'Oeuvres.............42
  Yakitori Chicken
  Easy Spring Rolls
  Grilled Tuna Sushi
  Miniature Fish Cakes
  Teriyaki Beef Cakes
  Lemon Ginger Dipping Sauce
  East-West Ginger Roll
  Pickled Baby Vegetables
  Toasted Pumpkin Seeds
  Chilli Dipping Sauce

Tea-Time Titbits 48
  Sweet Potato Cheese Scones
  Cinnamon Spirals
  Mango Waldorf Chicken Sandwiches
  Fruitcake Biscuits
  Apricot and Raspberry Tartlets
  Minted Cucumber Sandwiches

Scandinavian Smörgåsbord 52
  Scrambled Egg Avocados
  Sweet & Sour Pink Potatoes
  Smoked Haddock Croquettes with Tartare Sauce
  Open-Faced Gravadlax Sandwiches
  Lemon Cheese Pancakes
  Fancy Swedish Meatballs with Redcurrant Sauce
  Creamy Prawn Shells
  Orange Eggs
  Turkey Puffs with Cranberry Relish

English Nibbles **58**
Open-Faced Oyster Sandwiches
Curried Mustard Sauce
Whisky-Scented Bread Pudding
Chestnut-Stuffed Brussels
Farmhouse Sausage Rolls
Stilton-Walnut Grapes
Cheddar-Hazelnut Crackers
Miniature Scotch Eggs
Cider-Baked Lamb Cutlets

Champagne Brunch **64**
Mini-Sweetcorn 'Oysters' with Maple Syrup
Mushrooms on Toast
Melon Baskets
Poached Quails' Eggs in Cherry Tomatoes
Baby Bangers 'n' Mash
Hash-Stuffed Peaches
Devilled Ham in Eggs

French Hors d'Oeuvres **68**
Tarragon Cream Eggs
Garlic Courgette Curls
Black and White Florentines
Tapenade Toasts
Alsatian Cocktail Balls
Crudités with Aïoli
Spicy Stuffed Mushrooms
Finger Croque-Monsieurs
Prune Surprises
Fennel-Scented Olives

Chinese Dim Sum **74**
Sweet Fried Nuts
Spicy Meat in Chinese Leaves
Char Chiu Buns
Rice Croquettes with Hot Dipping Sauce
Hot Sweet and Sour Chicken Drumsticks
Prawn Toasts
Cantonese Almond Biscuits
Fruit with Cinnamon Dipping Sauce

A Formal Cocktail Party **80**
Nutty Apricot Mounds
Spiced Pistachio Brittle
Choux Buns with Smoked Trout Mousse
Dates with Cheese Stuffing
Crab and Prawn Palmiers
Devils on Horseback
Kabanos and Papaya Sticks

Indian Tiffin **84**
Split and Chick Pea Nibbles
Goanese Stuffed Courgettes
Spiced Chicken Samosas
Curried Broccoli Fritters with Coriander Dip
Almond Lamb Kebabs
Creamy Eggs in Bread Cases
Fruit-Topped Lemon Curd Tartlets
Candied Watermelon
Aubergine Sambal with Warm Chapati Strips

Italian Antipasto **90**
Italian Market Olives
Celery with Pesto
Scallop, Raddichio and Goat Cheese Bites
Caponata-Filled Tomatoes
Garlicky Mixed Tortellini
Stuffed Eggs Tomato
Deep-Fried Polenta Puffs with Spinach Dip
Fuselli Crunchies
Crostini with Sicilian Sardine Paste

The Perfect Picnic **96**
Avocado and Carrot Squares
Prawn and Cucumber Bowls
Creole Chicken Wings
Tabbouleh in Chicory Cups
Beef and Smoked Ham Cigars
Chocolate-Dipped Fruit
Lemon Squares

Southeast Asian Delights **100**
Prawn Crackers
Lamb and Chicken Saté with Peanut Sauce
Beef Dumplings with Mango Dip
Stuffed Squid Packets
Spiced Baby Sweetcorn
Sunshine Mix

Banana Lime Tarts
Vegetable Lettuce Rolls
Lychee-Pineapple Bites

Afro-Carib Tastees **106**
Buttered Brazil Chips
Caribbean Jerky
Beef, Coconut and Peanut Grills
Egg and Bacon Bundles
Deep-Fried Banana Kebabs with Lemon Sauce
Aruba Salt Cod Cakes with Avocado
Pineapple Muffins with Jamaica Pork
Jamaican Crab Dip with Sweet Potato Crisps
Cheese-and-Mango Biscuits
Nevis Fruit Bakes

A Children's Party **112**
Biscuit-Cutter Sandwiches
Frankfurter Boats
Quick Child-Sized Pizzas
Peanut Butter and Chocolate Bars
Piggy Back Potatoes
Old-Fashioned Potato Doughnuts

American Snacks **116**
Citrus Mixed Lettuce Cups
Spicy Peanut Spread
Vegetable Balls with Sweet Tomato Dip
Miniature Reuben Sandwiches
Potato Skins and Soured Cream
Southwestern Corn Muffins with Chilli
Individual Oysters Rockefeller
Maine Blueberry Chewies

Mexican Botanas **122**
Melon and White Cheese Sticks
Yucatan Sweetcorn Dip
Salsa-Stuffed Artichoke Bottoms
Picadillo with Nachos
Poor Man's Fish Puddings
Acapulco Seviche on Sticks
Sopaipillas
Sweet Potatoes with Guacamole
Mexicali Popcorn

Barbecued Bites **128**
Classic American Barbecued Burgers
Prawns in Bacon
Glazed Ribs
Garlic Vegetables on a Stick
Grilled Herbed Corn-on-the-Cob
Pecan Pie Squares

Raise Your Glasses **132**
Spirit-Free Thirst Quenchers
Old-Fashioned Spiced Lemonade
Sunshine Orangeade
Classic Lemon Barley Water
Sparkling Virgin Marys
Watermelon Slush
Tropical Blush
Exotic Fruit Flips
Gingered Apple Zinger
Hot Drinks and Punches
The Bishop
Hot Buttered Rum
Tom & Jerry
Viennese Glühwein
Yuletide Glögg
New England Mulled Cider
Wines and Champagne Coolers
Spanish Sangria
Strawberry Delight Punch
Louisiana Mint Cooler
Planter's Wine Punch
Henley Special
Pink Shocker
Spirited Encounters
Old-Fashioned Eggnog
Pitcher Moscow Mules
Caribbean Spritzer Punch
Pitcher Piña Coladas
Mint Juleps
Mexican Spitfire

Index **142**

Acknowledgements **144**

The Joys of Finger Food

As any child will tell you, there's something instantly appealing about food you can eat with your fingers. Somehow, it just tastes deliciously different, succulent and appetising. It's also the perfect food for entertaining – *al fresco* in the garden, on the patio or by the pool, or, indeed, within the home. Yet, despite these obvious pluses, until now this sort of food has always been seen as limited, at least in terms of the potential variety of dishes involved. Nothing could be further from the truth, as just a quick glance at what follows will show.

Recipes from across the world

In *Finger Food*, you will find 160 mouth-wateringly different recipes for delicious dishes, selected from the full range of the world's great culinary traditions and cuisines. What they all have in common is one single factor – they can all be picked up with the fingers and eaten. Some are simply bites – something pleasurable to be popped into the mouth quickly, to tantalize the tastebuds before vanishing, to be followed, you hope, by more of the same. Others are more substantial – three- or four-bite tit-bits for hearty eaters, ranging from such traditional favourites as miniature croque monsieurs, Scotch eggs with a difference, bangers and mash and individual bread puddings to more elegant and sophisticated fare, such as stuffed artichoke hearts, individual salmon roulades, cider lamb cutlets, ceviche on sticks and smoked haddock croquettes.

Taste, eye-appeal and ease both of preparation and consumption were the main guidelines in deciding what dishes to include.

Immediately following this introduction, you'll find some clear, concise advice on how to plan your finger-food entertaining so that it really entertains – but the over-riding principle I've followed carefully throughout is to select attractive dishes that can be prepared by even a relative culinary novice – and ruthlessly eliminated any that, when they were tested, involved elaborate complications and extended preparation times. For finger food is convenience food – it's food that should be as quick, easy and straightforward to prepare as it should be to eat.

Even given these criteria, choosing what to include – and what to leave out – was still a daunting task. What I've aimed to do is to include as wide a selection of dishes as possible – something to suit even the most finicky of tastes. For this reason, I have not scorned traditional favourites, such as dates with cream cheese, devils on horseback, stuffed and pickled eggs, Swedish meatballs and prawns wrapped in bacon. A whole host of hungry people over the years have shown their worth. However, I've livened them with a number of special touches of my own, while I've also introduced what I hope you will find an absorbing and attractive range of less familiar dishes, drawing on the rich variety of the world's cookery traditions. I hope, too, that, in all the recipes, you will find deliciously different tastes and ideas that you may not have encountered before.

In all, 14 different regional cuisines are featured, each treated individually in its own separate chapter. From Europe, I've included examples from north, south, east and west – from the calculated contrasts of savoury and sour favoured by Scandinavian and Russian cooks to classics from France and Italy, replete

with the unabashed flavours of garlic and the other herbs that dominate both these great cuisines. Greece and the Near East have contributed their own savours of lemon and thyme, while, from Britain, there are dishes utilizing a whole range of traditional ingredients, in particular meat, fruit and cheese.

From further afield, I've introduced a taste of the Orient, with a succession of unhackneyed delights from China, SouthEast Asia and Japan. India, too, is represented, through the subtle and varied marriage of spices that gave rise to our term "curried". I've used these, in very different ways, to transform an aubergine dip, broccoli fritters, creamed egg and almond lamb kebabs. Nor have I neglected the assertive bite of peppers, lemongrass and lime – or the smooth sweet and sour and peanut sauces. You'll find I make full use of their boundless potential.

Finally, looking towards the New World, I've chosen examples of the best and most characteristic of the area's finger food. From Mexico, for instance, I've borrowed heavily from tradition, featuring such staples as beans and corn, enlivened and refined through clever use of spices and such national treasures as rich dark chocolate and the mellow smoothness of ripe avocado. As for the United States, too long

billed as the home of fast food and dulled flavours, I've drawn on the rich diversity of its multi-faceted culinary inheritance. You'll see how echoes of Middle Europe, Mexico, France, Italy, the Far East and Britain have all added their resonance to native produce, such as pecans, blueberries, potatoes and pastrami.

Entertaining the finger-food way

Nor is this all. For that special occasion, I've devised seven self-contained recipe sections, in which carefully selected finger-food dishes have been brought together to suit a range of practical purposes. These include a stand-up supper, a children's party, formal cocktails, a traditional tea-party, a champagne brunch, a picnic and a barbeque. For finger-food entertaining is a hallowed culinary tradition over the generations, countless cooks have devised ingenious ways of preparing and serving such food without fuss. Today, western cooks have added their own fillip to these classic dishes, while, at the same time, the influences of other culinary cultures have become part and finger-food parcel of our parties and celebrations. The choice is yours, so turn the pages and pass the napkins – it's time to let your fingers do the choosing.

Hosting a Finger Food Party

If, in common with many people, you are too busy to entertain on any major scale, much as you might like to, or you just don't have sufficient space to make formal entertaining practical, then finger food is your answer. After all, the main object of any party is for you to enjoy yourself as much as your guests; any meal that puts you in a fluster from the moment the invitations are issued to the time your guests eventually leave is not really worth the time and trouble it involves. The point of entertaining is to enjoy what you are doing when you do it, not after the event.

While finger food certainly makes entertaining easier, it does not do away with the need to think ahead and pre-plan. What I intend to do here is to provide you with some useful tips and hints to set you on the right path to successful entertaining, so that you can make the most of the occasion, regardless of its scale or size.

Let's party

In common with any form of party, finger-food entertaining needs some prior thought. Right at the start, for instance, you need to think of not just whom you are going to invite, but of how many there will be; you also need to think of what you can serve, not forgetting the drinks to go with it, and what sort of atmosphere you want your party to have. As far as the last point is concerned, it all boils down to two simple words – formal or informal. This, too, is where finger food scores, since it enables you to combine the best elements of both approaches to entertaining.

The constraints of modern living mean that most of us cannot boast a dining table fit for a banquet; this means that, in reality, it is difficult to entertain more than, say, eight or so people to a formal sit-down meal without off-putting trouble and fuss. Yet these supposedly 'awkward' gatherings are often the jolliest of all – you can mix people who know each other with new faces with confidence in the result. A finger-food party enables you to indulge yourself and your guests by freeing both you and them from the constraints of formal etiquette. For one thing, it gives your guests the freedom of movement that is obviously denied to them at a sit-down meal. For another, it enables you to display more variety in your cooking, the chances being that you will produce food to suit every taste.

Planning in advance

Though food and drink feature high in the calculations for any finger-food party, there are several preliminaries that you should think about even in advance of these two essentials. Do you want to entertain at lunch-time, say, or in the evening? Will the party be held indoors or outside? If outside in the evening, considerations such as lighting (candles, torches or lamps) and noise (consider your neighbours) are both factors you must take into consideration. Will food and drink be served exclusively outside, or is it more convenient to dispense them from the kitchen or a living room? Bear in mind, too, if you are entertaining *al fresco*, that you should make sure your guests know this in advance – sweaters and jackets, even if unnecessary in the event, are always a wise precaution, as is suitable footwear – flat or wide-heeled shoes, rather than stillettos!

Tables versus trays

Dictated by season, time of day and plain ease of operation, indoor parties are by far the easiest to cater for on the whole. Here, your chief problems will be the size and position of rooms, which may pose both limitations on the number of people you can entertain without a crush – as well as providing you with logistical problems in ensuring everyone gets enough to eat and drink.

A home with small reception rooms and a downstairs kitchen, for example, does not permit the same ease of movement as does one with kitchen and entertainment area on the same floor. In the former instance, guests may pack themselves into one room – usually the one in which you have set out the food and drink – or leak out to find themselves marginally comfortable perches in the hall, stairs or elsewhere. It is in situations such as this that a traffic-jam – a recognizeable and avoidable danger at any finger-food party – can develop, as guests barricade the food tables or the bar, leaving others short of nourishment. One solution here is to segregate the drink from the food – try placing the former at the other end of the room from the latter, or have a welcoming tray of drinks on hand to greet your guests on arrival, with refills positioned elsewhere. You can also ask early arrivals to circulate with a bottle or two as the party hots up – close friends will not mind this, while, for a newcomer, it is an excellent way of helping him or her to break the ice and get acquainted.

Help yourself!

The whole essence of a finger-food party, however, is that guests should be able to help themselves as much as possible. So, rather than send trays of food around the rooms, it helps to set up some static food points ranged around them. This means that patrolling the food platters is important. It does not take long for attractively arranged canapes, sandwiches and finger salads to look as if the barbarian hordes have been raiding them. You need to keep the platters recharged. Remember here that nothing looks as unappetizing as new offerings placed willy-nilly beside tired old ones, which have made the rounds of the party half a dozen times or more. Careful eliminating, rearranging and maybe a swift trimming with a new garnish can give a lift to any plate as it re-emerges for another turn around the floor.

Remember, too, to keep some food back for late arrivals. Nothing is more embarrassing than watching late-comers fend for themselves, as they grimly pick through platters of messy, fingered food.

Lift your glass

What you are going to serve to drink demands as much advance planning as the food. Though this may sound obvious, check and clean glasses well before the party – and make sure you have enough, allowing for inevitable breakages. Decide on what drinks you are going to offer and then think how best to serve them – from a fixed bar, or by leaving an assortment of bottles and glasses scattered around the rooms, so that your guest can help themselves. Remember, too, to have a plentiful supply of mineral water and other soft drinks on hand – some non- or low-alcohol wine or beer is a good idea as well.

With white wine, the problem is keeping bottles chilled. Here, make use of the bath and/or bathroom sink. Fill them with ice – you can buy ice in quantity at most supermarkets – and a half-dozen or more bottles. This will provide you with the necessary reserve and the ice can be recharged at intervals. If you are serving red wine, remember to uncork the bottles well in advance to let the wine breathe. If you are serving Champagne or a sparkling wine, remember that bubbles actually tend to make people thirstier; it's vital to have something else on hand to cope with this.

However, it is at finger-food parties that punches, hot and cold, come into their own. There is something particularly celebratory about the vibrant colours of summer punches gleaming through glass bowls and steaming mugs of their winter equivalents.

It is a mistake to look upon a punch as a simple concoction, a kind of pot luck made from whatever drinks one likes oneself, or what happens to be in the drinks cupboard. True, it does mean that mixing can be done in large quantities, eliminating the need for several bottles on the go at one time. But it should be made following a recipe, like any good dish, straying neither towards becoming a knockout potion or a diluted imitation of the genuine article. If you are afraid that your guests may enjoy your creation *too* much, serve an alternative, non-alcoholic option. This is always a good idea, both for drivers and the health- and diet-conscious, and by providing a real composed punch instead of simply mineral water or fruit juice, you have not demoted them to second-class revellers.

For a summer punch, eliminate the bother of endless ice cubes – which tend to disappear into glasses anyway while serving – begin ahead. Fill small bowls or ice trays without the cube dividers, with water and freeze. Decant the ice blocks and store in the freezing compartment until you need them. Repeat until you have a comfortable supply. Place the first ice blocks in the punch bowls and large jugs before adding the mixture itself, but then add new blocks throughout the party as needed. For a more elegant touch, retain the ice cubes, but make them from filtered water (to reduce clouding) and plant a small flower in each cube space before filling.

Standing Comfortably?

The sun is out – or the lamps are lit in the drawing room. The punch is glistening in the bowl, the tables are laden with luscious titbits – or the platters and trays are arranged and ready to make the rounds. The stage is set for a relaxed celebration – or have you left your guests to juggle with the last problem?

If you have opted to let your friends help themselves from a table or tables, you will of course, and out of necessity, supply plates and napkins, arranged at the end of each food table. This will allow them to take several different finger foods at once, composing either a first course, or a first helping of their meal. This cuts down crowding, and allows the guests to see the choices on offer and to pace themselves accordingly.

Whether you choose china or paper plates depends on the formality of the occasion, the numbers and the washing-up facilities. In either case, avoid full size dinner plates which are far too unwieldy. Personally I feel real plates are worth the effort since they look more attractive to begin with and far less battered and unappetizing at the end. There are, however, some lovely sturdy paper plates on offer. If you decide in favour of paper plates, supply two to two-and-one-half times as many plates as there are guests; this will allow a change-over for particularly messy or collapsed ones. Regular checking to dispose of any used paper plates is also useful. If serving desert separately, you will need to plan accordingly.

Napkins are almost invariably made of paper – cloth becomes too much of an encumbrance without a seat at a table. For dainty teas and formal cocktails, elegant little napkins are available. Otherwise, it is a good idea to buy large dinner napkins, since they help keep your fingers clean. Good-sized napkins should also be offered if the food is being circulated among the guests.

Finally, more important than the style of the surroundings, the placement of the utensils, and the quality of the food and drink, is your good humour. Much of this comes, of course, from knowing that everything is as well-planned and organised as it can be, but it also comes from an innate satisfaction in giving pleasure. To entertain well does *not* mean that the party-giver needs to be personally entertaining. The entertainment is hopefully provided by the guests themselves, in an ambiance created by a sympathetic and imaginative host, who cares enough to make sure they enjoy themselves – in this case, right down to their fingertips.

Secrets of Garnishing

In the days when Escoffier and Brillat Savarin ruled the kitchen, garnishes were highly elaborate affairs. Composed of several ingredients and arranged in patterns dictated by tradition and the restrictions of *haute cuisine*, they were almost mini-courses in themselves and often demanded as much preparation time as the dishes they complemented. Spontaneity and a light touch were hardly keynotes of classic garnitures; they were tests of a kitchen's command of the finest points of *la table*. Christened with the names of countries, regions, towns, national heroes and society notables, they were catalogued with rigorous attention to detail.

Thus any dish *à la financière* was bound by convention to contain chicken or veal quenelles, cock's combs and kidneys, mushrooms and shredded truffles, with stoned and blanched olives and freshwater crayfish as optional extras. *Escallopes à la Marigny* were sure to be surrounded by glazed potato balls and small artichoke hearts filled with creamed corn, accompanied by a sauce of white wine and veal stock, while any shellfish styles *Américaine* boasted slices of crayfish or lobster tails served in a rich reduction of shellfish stock, tomatoes, wine and brandy. Even a dish as homely as *Poulet Bonne Femme* (literally 'chicken good

woman', the good woman being the house-keeper/cook) demanded an arrangement of small potatoes pared into ovals, baby onions and mushrooms.

With the passage of time there was some allowance for deviation, but that too was codified into the litany of acknowledged garnitures.

A dish *à la ancienne* could take one of three opulent forms, ranging from a fantasy of chicken forcemeat balls and truffles with lamb sweetbreads and crayfish, to pastry boats filled with soft roes and *sauce Normande*, accompanied by olive-shaped truffles, mushrooms and those ubiquitous crayfish. *Orientale, Parisienne, Niçoise or Hongoise* on a menu could all admit the possibility of variety, but for the most part, the gods of taste – both sensual and stylistic – would brook little invention. The designation of a garnish was a statement of intent.

Today, thank goodness, all that has changed. Only in creaking establishment restaurants are escape the leavening influence of *nouvelle cuisine* and healthier eating habits. Our preoccupation with food was revived and we gave equal importance to presentation and flavour, far less to social snobbisms like numerous courses and extravagant ingredients. The new rules for garnishes - if anything as inflexible as rules can be claimed for the ever-changing inspirational flourishes found on salads, hors d'oeuvres, soups, casseroles, roasts and desserts - abandoned obviousness for subtlety, and exoticism and extravagance for suitability of purpose. Today garnishes are back in fashion, and be they traditional, or your own invention, the object is not to overwhelm the diner but to tantalize the eye and the palate - to make the dish even more visually and gastronomically pleasing than it would be without it. If the garnish is redundant, then it is a waste of time and effort to use it.

Some of the simplest and most sucessful pair

garnish and dish are based on long acknow-ledged complementary flavours – herbs such as mint, rosemary and coriander with lamb, tar-ragon with chicken, dill with fish, and chillies and coriander with Eastern dishes, have always made good marriages. Fruits or vegetables with meats or fish – apples and plums with pork, oranges and peaches with duck, cranberries with turkey, lemon with fish, pineapples with gammon, spring onions with eggs and fish, cucumber with salmon, turned mushrooms with roasted meats, gerkins with pâtés – also make classic partners. Rather than simply throwing the fruit or vegetable slices uncere-moniously around the featured food however, the artistic chef has turned them into art forms, sculpting stars, roses, brushes, twists and coils to add more texture and interest to com-binations that otherwise would be taken for granted.

Other garnishes, however, are chosen as much for visual and textual contrast as for flavour: pastel prawns or red pepper flowers against creamy avocado mousse: sliced or dev-illed eggs on crunchy greens or vegetables; fancy-cut cheese hearts and stars with fresh fruit; cucumber, orange slices and strawberries in a Pimms Cup. Such pairing demands a sensi-tive eye, since it is easy enough to overload a dish with 'improvements' that only serve to dis-tract or disguise.

Most of the garnishes used in this book are very simple to make, requiring only a sharp knife and a steady hand. A *canelle* or grooved citrus parer is useful for decking rinds on fruit and vegetables, though a vegetable peeler will produce acceptable if less fine results. Other utensils that may come in handy are fancy cut-ters (for vegetables and cheese) and a piping bag (for whipped cream, soft cheeses and mousse decorations). A melon baller can be used to shape colourful watermelon, ogen or cantaloupe balls, or to mould soft cheeses into spheres rolled in chopped nuts or parsley. While such delights are included in this book as noteworthy finger foods in their own right, they can also be enrolled as garnishes to enliv-en other dishes.

There are many more time-consuming garnish-es in the repertoire of the modern chef. Fried greenery such as celery leaves and parsley, or the classic small baskets of grafted potatoes, to hold medleys of meat or vegetables, put the deep-frier to elegant use. Aspic can be mould-ed or cut into delightfully decorative forms. Butters can be flavoured and coloured before being rolled and sliced, or made into balls or curls. Red pepper, caper, herb and orange but-ters all make attractive and delicious additions to offer alongside tiny bread rolls or positioned inside baby baked potatoes.

The Thais have a marvellous tradition of intricateley carved fruit and vegetables, used as centrepieces of the meal or arranged on plat-ters of food as they are presented. Small swim-ming fish, carved from diakon radish and car-rot, will decorate a plate of simple gingered scallops; large melons and gourds, embellished with whole scenes from Buddhist legend, domi-nate diplomatic banquets and hotel buffets. Perhaps such exceptional works have crossed over from the culinary to the truly visual arts. The term 'garnish' hardly seems adequate to describe the glory of their finest and largest expression.

So the world of garnishes is a wide one, and the ingenuity of chefs and magazine stylists, who influence so much of home entertaining, are pushing it ever wider. But beware of guild-ing the lily; don't let the plethora of vegetable flourishes staring at you from every cookery photograph or restaurant plate persuade you that they are indispensable. Garnishes are tools to be used at your discretion, and restraint can show as much artistry as display.

Simple Leaf and Flower Garnishes

These decorative devices are the least complicated possible and, except for the flowers, of course, in all shades of green. They are most effective when used in conjunction with elaborate finger food which will benefit from non-competitive garnishing, and with salad-style hors d'oeuvres containing a number of ingredients.

Leaves — Uses

Leaves	Uses
Celery leaves	cheeses or dishes containing celery
Watercress sprigs	all salads and meats
Lettuce ruffles	almost all savoury dishes
Lollo rosso, frisé, oak leaf, endive, vine leaves	cheeses, Middle Eastern and Mediterranean-style dishes
Scented geranium leaves	fruit-based dishes, sweet dishes
Herb sprigs, parsley, mint, thyme, rosemary, dill, fennel, chives, coriander, sage, chervil	all savoury dishes; mint with some sweets.
Parsley, mint, thyme, rosemary, dill, fennel chives, coriander	general and British-style dishes; Mediterranean-style dishes; Northern and Eastern European; Oriental, Indian, Mexican

Flowers — Uses

Flowers	Uses
Nasturtium, Polyanthas, chrysanthemum, borage, lavender	salad dishes

Fruit and Vegetable Garnishes

These are colourful, assertive garnishes, and should be used with discretion. Try to pair these un-tampered-with vegetables and fruits with the cuisines usually associated with them, and which may have been used in the preparation of the dishes themselves. Use restraint in mixing colours; don't over-extend your visual palette.

Garnish — Uses

Garnish	Uses
Citrus slices (orange, lemon, lime)	as colour contrast/complement to savoury dishes and salads; drinks and some sweet dishes
Pineapple slices	complement to savoury dishes, especially Oriental and Caribbean; sweet dishes and drinks
Kumquat slices	a particular complement to Oriental and Indian dishes, savoury and sweet
Starfruit slices	particularly useful for Oriental and Caribbean savoury and sweet dishes
Raw mushrooms; red onion rings; red, green and yellow pepper rings	highly colourful garnishes; particularly useful on dullish or plain coloured savoury dishes. Onion rings associated with Scandinavian and Eastern European cuisines; peppers with Mediterranean cuisines
Olives (green or black, plain or stuffed, whole or sliced)	all savoury dishes; usually associated with Middle Eastern, Mediterranean, Mexican and American cuisines
Cherry tomatoes, tomato slices	all savoury dishes and salads, especially with Scandinavian, Eastern European, British and American cuisines
Grapes (red or white)	salads, some savoury and sweet dishes
Soft fruits (redcurrant branchlets, cherries on stem, strawberries)	sweet dishes, drinks

More Elaborate Garnishes

The same holds true for these ornamentally-cut and prepared fruits and vegetables as for plain garnishes only more so. Use them to highlight a plate of finger food or the occasional individual item itself, but don't overdo it. As in conversation, here economy is the soul of culinary wit.

Garnishing Tricks Suitable for Both Fruit and Vegetables

Fans – Kiwi, gherkin or cucumber

Gherkin or cucumber fans look well and make a tasty complement to pâté-based finger foods, as well as eggs and salady hors d'oeuvres. Kiwi fans are better teamed with sweets or fruit-based nibbles.

1. *First peel kiwi fruit; proceed with gherkin or cucumber as it is. Using a sharp knife, cut kiwi fruit into quarters; gherkin or cucumber in half. Cut off the bottom of the cucumber half to remove the seeds.*
2. *Cut cucumber on the diagonal into 8cm/3in pieces. Make about 8 very thin diagonal slices on each piece, not quite cutting through to the far edge.*
3. *Cut about 5 slices lengthways along kiwi fruit or gherkin, stopping short of the end. Gently ease apart the slices, making a 'fan'.*

Curls – Carrots/cucumber – orange, lemon and lime rind

1. *For carrots, first thinly peel off the skin. For cucumbers and citrus fruits, use the skin. Use a vegetable peeler to peel off long, thin strips vertically from the cucumber or carrot, and in a circular motion from the fruit. (Take only the coloured zest from citrus fruits, leaving all white pith behind.)*
2. *Wind the strips into a tight coil and pack into ice cube trays. Cover with iced water and chill for 8 hours or overnight.*
3. *Uncoil the strips and shake off excess moisture. Use the vegetable curls to decorate savoury dishes and the fruit coils as a garnish for drinks and sweet dishes.*

Deckled slices – Cucumber or courgette; orange, lemon or lime

1. *Using a canelle knife, run the blade at intervals down the length of the peel or rind, giving it a striped appearance.*
2. *Slice the fruit or vegetable as thinly as possible, to show off its translucency and the deckled edge.*
3. *(Optional) The cucumber slices can be dusted with paprika; the lemon peel can be pressed into chopped parsley or poppy seeds.*

16

Cones – Cucumber; orange, lemon or lime

These can be used on any of the dishes listed for twists, and they are particularly suited to platters of finger sweets, which are often difficult to garnish. Decorate the cones with stems of mint or scented geranium.

1. *Cut the vegetable or fruit into thin slices, as above. Using a sharp knife, slit to the centre.*
2. *Fold one cut edge over the other, forming a cone or funnel.*
3. *Place a 'stamen' in the middle of the cone, such as a tiny sprig of mint, dill or parsley. In addition, capers or a cherry slice can be used for citrus fruit, depending on whether it is used to garnish a savoury or sweet dish.*

Concertina – radish

Radishes have a distinctive peppery flavour which complements cold meats, fish and vegetable terrines and platters, and composed salads. They are particularly prized by French and Middle European cooks, but can overpower more delicate dishes.

1. *Use long radishes for this garnish. Using a sharp knife, finely trim the ends, then make 6-8 cuts horizontally along the radish, stopping short of cutting through.*
2. *Drop the radishes into iced water and leave for 1 hour. When you remove them they will have opened out like a concertina.*

Vegetable Garnishes

Brushes – Celery or spring onions

These are popular as nibbles in themselves and look good in bunches surrounding salads or meat-, fish-, or egg-based finger foods.

1. *Scrub celery stalks and cut into 5cm/2in lengths. Trim spring onion roots and cut tops so that the onion is about 10cm/4in long.*
2. *With a sharp knife, cut the length of the spring onion to within 3cm /1¼ in of the root end. Turn the onion slightly and make another fine cut; continue 3-4 times. Cut the length of the celery stalk almost to the base.*
3. *Drop the vegetables into iced water and chill for 1 hour. When you remove them they will have curled attractively.*

Star – Tomato

Tomatoes are highly adaptable, and their sweet acidity equally complements meats, vegetables, fish and eggs. As a garnish, they are much in demand because of their cheerful colour, and can lift many an otherwise dull dish. However, avoid using tomatoes with everything, the resort of the unimaginative. Use with discretion and flair.

1. *Using a sharp knife, cut a small or cherry tomato almost in half, stopping just short of the bottom. Turn the tomato and cut across the slice, into quarters, again stopping short of the bottom. Repeat two more times, cutting across the quarters and ending with the tomato cut into eighths.*
2. *Gently ease open the tomato star.*

17

Rose – Radish

Use radish roses to garnish the same foods as pompoms. While red radishes look very pretty in this guise, two-tone white-and-red French radishes lend an extra dimension.

1. *Using a sharp knife, make 5-6 just overlapping slices around the circumference of a radish, from the base end towards the stalk, making sure you do not cut through the radish.*
2. *Drop the radish(es) into a bowl of iced water and chill for 30 minutes. When you remove the radish(es), it will have opened slightly; repeat the cutting process on the inner white part and chill in the water for a further 30 minutes. When you remove it, it will have opened wider.*

Rose – Tomato skin

These make attractive and appealing garnishes. They are usually used sparingly as focal points on the edges of meat, fish or hors d'oeuvres platters, where they will not get in the way of eager guests or disappear from the arrangement.

1. *Use a firm, ripe medium-sized tomato and a sharp paring knife. Beginning at the non-stalk end, peel a very thin continuous strip of skin from the tomato, turning it with one hand as you carefully slice with the other. Round off at the stalk end.*
2. *Beginning with the stalk end, roll the skin around itself, flesh-side in. As you get towards the end, roll somewhat less tightly.*
3. *Ease the 'petals' into shape, and decorate with fresh mint or borage, if desired.*

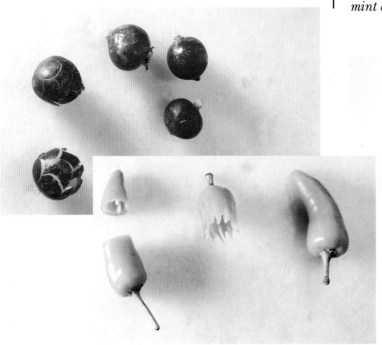

Bellflowers – Red or green chillies

Depending on the length and thinness of the chilli, the 'petals' of the bellflowers can be made longer and more curling. Raw chillies, deseeded, are best for finger foods, since they can be eaten – by the brave! Use on meat and salad hors d'oeuvres.

1. *Retain the sepal and stalk of the chilli(es). Using a sharp knife, cut off the long end, leaving about half the chilli. Use the sharp tip of the knife to clean out the seeds and core.*
2. *Take a pair of small, sharp scissors and cut 'V'-shaped pieces from around the chopped end, leaving a series of pointed 'petals'.*
3. *Drop the bellflowers into iced water and chill for 1-2 hours. When removed, they will have 'flowered'.*

Fruit Garnishes

Citrus julienne – Orange, lemon or lime

These fine hair-like shavings of peel can be scattered over punches and salads, or lend a pretty acidity to curried dishes and stir-fries. They also perk up citrus-based desserts.

1. *Use a vegetable peeler to shave off thin sections of zest from the fruit.*
2. *Use the sharp end of a knife to scrape any pith away from the back of the zest.*
3. *Trim the tops and bottoms of the zest, then cut the sections into very thin strips.*
4. *Blanch the julienne in boiling water for a few seconds, then drain and dry on kitchen paper.*

Knotted citrus slices – Orange, lemon or lime

These make attractive additions to the same foods as citrus twists and deckled slices.

1. With a sharp knife, cut the fruit in half. Cut a small slice from the bottom of the fruit to balance it.
2. Using a small paring knife, cut away a small strip of zest (about 5mm/½in) around the top edge of one half, stopping just before reaching the beginning. Try to make the strip fairly thin, leaving most of the pith on the flesh.
3. Tie a 'knot' with the strip, looping the end of the strip through the knot decoratively.
4. Cut off a slice with the knot, and repeat with the next slices and the other half, as needed.

Other Garnishes

Quarters or slices – Egg

These egg garnishes are attractive on open-faced sandwiches or on finger salads arranged in lettuce or chicory leaves.

1. Bring eggs to the boil; cook for 5 minutes. Take off the heat and allow to sit in the water for 20-25 minutes, depending on size. Plunge into cold water and leave until cool. Carefully peel.
2. Cut each egg into quarters with a knife, or into round slices with an egg slicer.
3. Lightly spread one side of a quarter or half an egg slice with mayonnaise; dip into or press on chopped parsley, chives or red or black lumpfish roe. Alternatively, sprinkle the egg slices with paprika.

Frosted fruit – White or black grapes; black- or red currants

Frosted fruit bunches are generally best used as a garnish on platters of finger desserts, although tiny bunches of frosted currants can be easily accommodated on individual sweets, particularly those with a creamy or mousse base.

1. Choose small clusters of grapes or currants. Beat an egg white in a bowl until frothy.
2. Brush the clusters or dip in a little of the beaten egg white.
3. Dredge the grapes or currants in caster sugar and leave on a rack to dry.

Fancy-cut shapes – Cheese or vegetable

Cheese shapes are especially good as a decoration on meat hors d'oeuvres or arranged attractively with celery brushes as a savoury. Use vegetable shapes to garnish salad and vegetable finger foods.

1. Cut not-too-crumbly cheese into slices (mild to medium Cheddar, Leicester, Emmental, Bleu d'Avergne, Sage Derby, Red Windsor, etc). Prepare the vegetables (carrots, cooked beetroot, green or red pepper) by cutting away extraneous matter. Peel and trim the carrots and beetroot; core and seed the peppers. Cut beetroot into rounds, carrot into thin slices, peppers into quarters.

2. Using tiny fancy vegetable cutters – in the shapes of stars, crescents, hearts, clubs, etc. – cut out shapes to decorate hors d'oeuvres, stuffed eggs, etc.

Mediterranean Mezze

The nations of the Eastern Mediterranean and North Africa, including Greece, with its romantic islands and the relatively new holiday destination of Turkey – all share common culinary influences. The cross-fertilisation is apparent in this bounteous spread, especially in the use of phyllo pastry, the popularity of lamb, artichokes, white salted cheese, tomatoes and pine kernels, and the sweetly astringent scents of lemon and mint. They possess a universal appeal when set out on a summery table and accompanied by plenty of light white wine or perhaps, pine-scented retsina.

Hummus-Filled Miniature Pittas

4 tbsp sesame seeds
2x 425g/15oz cans chick peas, drained
6 tbsp olive oil
6 tbsp fresh lemon juice
2 garlic cloves, chopped
Salt and black pepper

24 miniature cocktail-size pittas, slit open

To Garnish
Cucumber slices
Endive leaves
Black olives

illustrated on page 21

Makes about 25

Toast the sesame seeds in a frying pan over a medium heat until golden, stirring to colour evenly. Combine with the chick peas, oil, lemon juice, garlic, and salt and pepper to taste, in a food processor fitted with a metal blade. Process until smooth. Pour the hummus into a bowl and set aside for 3-4 hours, or preferably overnight, to allow the flavours time to blend.

Spoon the hummus into the pockets of the pittas and garnish each with the cucumber, endive and black olives.

Lemon-Scented Stuffed Vine Leaves

32 vine leaves in brine, drained
225g/8oz cooked long-grain white rice
5 tbsp olive oil
1 small onion, finely chopped
350g/12oz minced lamb, browned and drained

2 garlic cloves, finely chopped
1½ tsp dried mint
1 tsp dried oregano
60g/2oz curd cheese
2 tbsp pine kernels
Salt and black pepper
2 tsp fresh lemon juice
Twist of lemon, to garnish

illustrated on page 21

Makes 32

Soak the vine leaves in boiling water for 5 minutes; drain and rinse in cold water. Pat dry with kitchen paper.

Preheat the oven to 160°C/325°F/Gas Mark 3. Mix together the rice, 2 tablespoons olive oil, the onion, lamb, garlic, herbs, curd cheese, pine kernels and salt and pepper to taste. Take a small handful of the mixture and place in the centre of a vine leaf. Fold in the sides and roll up neatly. Repeat with the remaining leaves and filling mixture. As the vine leaves are stuffed and rolled, pack them into oiled baking dishes in a single layer.

Pour 150ml/¼ pint water over the rolls, then mix the remaining oil with the lemon juice and drizzle over the leaves.

Cover and bake for about 50 minutes. Cool in the liquid before serving. (The vine leaves may be kept, covered and chilled, for up to 3 days or they can be frozen.) Garnish with the twists of lemon.

Clockwise from the top: *hummus-filled miniature pittas, miniature shish kebabs, easy kebbeh, lemon-scented stuffed vine leaves.*

Spinach-Phyllo Triangles

1 small onion, chopped	Salt and black pepper
5 tbsp olive oil	2 eggs, beaten
675g/1½ lb fresh spinach, cooked and chopped	225g/8oz feta cheese, crumbled
1 tbsp chopped fresh dill	15 phyllo sheets
2 tbsp chopped fresh parsley	60-75g/2-2½oz butter, (melted)
30g/1oz raisins, soaked in water and drained	

illustrated on page 23

Makes about 20

Sauté the onion in 1 tablespoon oil until softened. Add the spinach, dill, parsley, raisins and salt and pepper to taste, and cook for a further 15 minutes, or until most of the moisture has evaporated. Transfer to a bowl and stir in the eggs and feta cheese until well-mixed.

(When using the phyllo, make sure to keep it covered with a damp cloth to keep it from drying.) Mix together the remaining oil and the melted butter in a bowl. Take 3 sheets of phyllo at one time, and brush each lightly with the fat before topping with the next. When the three are assembled, cut widthways into four strips. Place a tablespoon or so of the filling at the top of one strip and quickly fold into a triangle. Brush the remainder of the strip with the oil mixture and continue to fold, triangle fashion, until you reach the bottom of the strip. Repeat with the remaining strips; then repeat with the next batch of 3 phyllo sheets and so on until you have used up all the pastry and filling. Remember to cover the finished triangles with a damp cloth to prevent the pastry from drying out.

Preheat the oven to 190°C/375°F/Gas Mark 5. Place the triangles on lightly greased baking sheets, brush the triangles with a little of the oil mixture, and bake until the pastries are golden, about 20-30 minutes. Allow to cool slightly, and serve.

Feta-Filled Artichoke Hearts

120g/4oz feta cheese, cut into tiny cubes	2 tsp chopped fresh basil
1 tbsp bottled crema di peperoni (red pepper sauce)	Black pepper
	2x 450g/1 lb jars marinated artichoke hearts
2 tbsp extra virgin olive oil	150g/5oz prosciutto, cut into long strips

illustrated on page 25

Makes about 16-20

Combine the feta cheese, red pepper sauce, olive oil, basil and pepper to taste in a bowl and leave to macerate for several hours.

Drain the artichoke hearts thoroughly. Cut a thin slice off the base of each so that it will stand straight. Gently open the interior leaves of each artichoke heart and stuff the centre carefully with a teaspoon of the cheese mixture. Wind a strip of prosciutto around each heart and secure with a cocktail stick.

Artichoke and Tomato Barquettes

450g/1 lb plain flour	1 garlic clove, finely chopped
½ tsp dry mustard	10 sun-dried tomato halves in oil, drained and cut into small pieces
Salt and black pepper	
225g/8oz butter or margarine	
225g/8oz Emmental cheese, grated	½ tbsp chopped fresh basil
1 size-2 egg yolk	½ tbsp chopped fresh thyme
	90g/3oz ricotta cheese
Filling	250ml/8fl oz double cream
15g/½oz butter	2 eggs
1 small onion, chopped	90g/3oz Emmental cheese, grated
½ x 397g/14oz can artichoke hearts, drained and chopped	30g/1oz Parmesan cheese, grated

illustrated on page 25

Makes about 24

Combine the flour and mustard in a large bowl and add salt and pepper to taste. Cut the butter or margarine into small pieces and add to the bowl, then begin to work it into the flour with your fingertips. When you have rubbed in half of the butter, add the grated cheese and continue to rub in the butter and cheese until the mixture is crumbly. Add the egg yolk and enough cold water to bind into a dough. Shape into a ball, cover and chill for at least 1 hour. (The dough can be kept in the refrigerator for 4-5 days.)

Preheat the oven to 200°C/400°F/Gas Mark 6.

Spinach-Phyllo triangles.

Bring the dough back to room temperature, then roll it out on a lightly floured surface and use to line 24 boat-shaped tartlet moulds (barquettes), each 11.5 x 6cm (4½ x 2⅜in), or round tartlet moulds. Prick well. Bake the pastry shells blind, on a baking tray, for 12-15 minutes or until lightly golden and set. Cool, then gently remove the pastry shells from the moulds.

Lower the oven heat to 190°C/375°F/Gas Mark 5. To make the filling, melt the butter and sauté the onion until soft. Add the artichoke hearts and garlic and continue cooking until almost all moisture has evaporated. Remove from the heat. Stir half of the tomatoes into the mixture.

Beat the basil, thyme, ricotta cheese, cream and eggs together in a bowl. Stir in the cooked artichoke and tomato mixture and seasoning to taste, making sure they are well blended.

Line up the pastry shells on a baking tray and sprinkle the bottoms with half the grated Emmental and Parmesan cheeses. Cover with the artichoke and tomato mixture, then top with the remaining grated cheese. Garnish with the remaining tomato pieces.

Bake the barquettes for 8 minutes, then lower the heat to 160°C/325°F/Gas Mark 3 and bake for 20 minutes longer, or until the filling is set. Cool a little and serve immediately.

Easy Kebbeh

450g/1 lb minced beef	**Crust**
1 small onion, finely chopped	150ml/¼ pint tomato juice
¼ tsp ground cinnamon	350g/12oz fine bulgur
¼ tsp grated nutmeg	Salt
⅛ tsp ground cloves	½ tsp cayenne pepper
½ tsp black pepper	½ tsp ground cumin
120g/4oz shelled walnuts, chopped	½ tsp paprika
Lamb's lettuce (mache), to garnish	450g/1 lb lean minced beef
	3 tbsp slivered almonds
	120g/4oz butter, melted
	3 tbsp sunflower oil

illustrated on page 21

Makes 20-25

Fry the beef in a large frying pan until it is browned and crumbly. Add the onion and cook, stirring, for a further 10 minutes. Drain off the fat, and stir in the spices and walnuts. Set aside.

To make kebbeh crust, combine 175ml/6fl oz water, the tomato juice and bulgur in a food processor fitted with a metal blade. When thoroughly mixed, add the spices, half of the beef and salt to taste. Process until smooth, then repeat using the remainder of the beef. Turn the mixture on to a work surface lightly dusted with flour and knead with your hands, squeezing and pressing it a little at a time, until it has a paste-like consistency.

Preheat the oven to 200°C/400°F/ Gas Mark 6. Take half of the crust mixture and press it over the bottom of a 27.5cm/11in square or 30 x 20cm / 12 x 8in cake tin, making it as flat as possible. Spread over the cooked beef mixture, smoothing it evenly. Cover with the remainder of the crust mixture, patting it flat. Run a knife in diagonal lines through the kebbeh, then repeat the lines in the opposite direction, cutting the kebbeh into diamond shapes. Make sure that the knife cuts through the layers to the bottom of the pan.

Sprinkle the almonds on top and press in gently. Combine the melted butter and oil and brush over the kebbeh, making sure that the mixture penetrates into all the cuts. Bake for about 45 minutes, or until golden brown. Allow to cool slightly before carefully lifting out the kebbeh and separating it into individual diamond shaped pieces. Arrange on a platter and garnish with tufts of Lamb's lettuce.

Lentil and Courgette Patties

175g/6oz lentils, rinsed	2 tbsp finely chopped fresh parsley
1 small onion, finely chopped	2 egg yolks
2 garlic cloves, finely chopped	120g/4oz dry breadcrumbs
3 tbsp white wine vinegar	Oil for frying
6 tbsp olive oil	
1 medium tomato, seeded and chopped	**Dipping sauce**
Salt and black pepper	2 tbsp fresh lemon juice
2 small courgettes, grated	2 tbsp finely chopped fresh dill
1 tsp ground cumin	1 tbsp capers
1½ tsp ground coriander	150ml/¼ pint plain Greek-style yogurt

Makes about 15-20

First make the sauce: combine all the ingredients in a decorative bowl, cover and chill for at least 1 hour.

Combine the lentils and the onion in a large saucepan and add enough water to cover. Bring to the boil and simmer for 25 minutes; in the last five minutes, add the garlic. Meanwhile, whisk together the vinegar and oil in a bowl. Add the tomato, grated courgettes and add salt and pepper to taste.

Drain the lentils thoroughly, and stir into the courgette mixture. Add the cumin, coriander and parsley. Beat the egg yolks lightly before stirring into the mixture, together with 4 tablespoons of the breadcrumbs.

Scoop out tablespoons of the mixture and shape them into patties about 1cm/½ in thick. Spread the remaining breadcrumbs on a plate and coat the patties on all sides.

Fry in batches in hot oil until golden and drain on kitchen paper. Serve warm with the sauce.

Miniature Shish Kebabs

900g/2 lb lamb fillet
3 tbsp tahini paste
3 tbsp sunflower oil
150ml/¼ pint fresh lemon
    juice
2 garlic cloves, chopped
1 fresh green chilli, seeded
    and finely chopped

2 tbsp chopped fresh
    coriander
1 tsp ground cumin

Dipping Sauce
2 tbsp prepared mint sauce
300ml/½ pint plain Greek-
    style yogurt

illustrated on page 21

Makes 20-25

Left: *artichoke and tomato barquettes.*
Right: *feta-filled artichoke hearts.*

Cut the lamb into 1cm/½in cubes and place them in a shallow bowl.

Mix together the tahini paste, oil, lemon juice, garlic, fresh chilli, coriander and cumin, and pour over the meat. Allow to marinate for at least 3 hours, mixing occasionally.

Preheat the grill to high.

Thread the cubes of lamb on to small wooden skewers. Grill for about 20 minutes, turning and brushing with the marinade from time to time. Meanwhile, make the sauce by combining the ingredients in a small bowl.

Serve the kebabs hot with the sauce.

Russian Zakuski

Russian cooking is adventurous and lively – and evokes thoughts of delicious ingredients such as smoked salmon, caviar and vodka. The range of Russia's imaginative cooking is represented here by 'little bites' or zakuski. Potatoes make two attractive appetisers, while cabbage and beetroot surprise with fillings unprosaic. Toast the company with pepper vodka – they'll all be comrades by the end of the evening!

Stuffed Baby Beetroot

700g/1½ lb bottled pickled baby beetroot	*60g/2oz cream cheese*
	30g/1oz butter
1 smoked trout, skinned and boned (about 150g/5oz)	*½ tsp horseradish cream*
	Salt and black pepper

illustrated on page 27

Makes 30-35

Drain the beetroot thoroughly. Cut a small slice off the base of each beetroot so that it stands upright. With a small sharp knife, cut a deep V-shaped hole in the top of each beetroot. Set aside.

Put the trout, cream cheese, butter and horseradish cream in a food processor or blender and process until smooth. Season to taste. (The filling and beetroot can be prepared up to this point and then left separately, covered, in the refrigerator overnight if wished.)

Put the trout mixture into a piping bag fitted with a star tube and pipe decoratively into each of the prepared beetroot.

New Potatoes with Caviar

30 new or baby potatoes	*60g/2oz black lumpfish roe*
Sunflower oil	*60g/2oz red salmon roe*
Salt	*3 tbsp finely chopped fresh chives*
150ml/¼ pint soured cream	

Makes 30

Preheat the oven to 190°C/375°F/Gas Mark 5. Rub the skins of the potatoes with oil and salt lightly. Put the potatoes in the oven and bake for 20-25 minutes, or until soft.

Carefully split open the potatoes and press gently to plump out the flesh. Top each potato with a piped ribbon or dab of soured cream. Drop ½ teaspoon of lumpfish roe on 15 of the potatoes and ½ teaspoon of salmon roe on the remaining potatoes. Sprinkle each lightly with chopped chives and serve immediately.

Left: *finger cabbage rolls.* Top right: *stuffed baby beetroot.* Bottom right: *curd cheese and ham piroshki.*

Finger Cabbage Rolls

1 large cabbage
30g/1oz butter
2 onions, chopped
1x425g/15oz can beef
  consommé
2 tbsp honey
3 tbsp fresh lemon juice
Lemon slices, to garnish

Filling
450g/1 lb minced beef
60g/2oz raisins
45g/1½ oz long-grain rice
1 medium-sized onion,
  grated
1 egg
Salt and black pepper

illlustrated on page 27

Makes 30

Bring a large pan of water to the boil and immerse the cabbage in it. Simmer for 10–15 minutes, then remove the cabbage from the water and carefully peel off 15 large leaves. (Repeat the process of boiling the water and simmering the cabbage, if necessary, to loosen 15 leaves in all.) Cut the leaves in half lengthways, trimming off the tough central rib. Set aside.

In a flameproof casserole, melt the butter and sauté the onions until soft and golden. Add enough water to the consommé to make 600ml/1 pint; pour over the onions and bring to the boil. Turn down the heat and leave to simmer for 15 minutes.

Meanwhile make the cabbage rolls: in a bowl, combine all the filling ingredients, mixing well. Place a small spoonful on a half cabbage leaf, fold in the sides and bottom and roll up. Secure with a wooden cocktail stick. Repeat with all the half leaves. (The stock and cabbage rolls can be made ahead to this point and kept separately.)

Place the rolls in the stock, spooning it over. Cover and cook over a low heat for 1 hour.

Combine the honey and lemon juice and trickle over the rolls; continue to cook for a further 30 minutes over a very low heat.

Drain the rolls with a slotted spoon, remove the sticks and serve warm or at room temperature, garnished with lemon slices.

Potato Croquettes with Surprise Filling

1kg/2¼ lb cooked peeled
  potatoes
5 tbsp single cream
Salt and black pepper
Pinch of cayenne pepper
1 tsp garlic purée
2 egg yolks, beaten
2 whole eggs, beaten with a
  little water
Dry breadcrumbs
Oil for deep frying

Fresh chives, to garnish

Filling
175g/6oz minced pork
1 tsp ground allspice
12 ready-to-eat plump
  stoned prunes, chopped
120ml/4fl oz double cream
2 slices of bread, crusts
  removed, shredded into
  crumbs

Makes about 16

Mash the potatoes thoroughly and mix together with the cream, seasoning to taste, cayenne pepper, garlic purée and egg yolks. Set aside.

To make the filling, fry the pork until browned and crumbly. Add the allspice and prunes and stir for a few minutes, then drain off the fat. In a saucepan, cook the cream and breadcrumbs over medium heat to make a thick paste. Stir the pork mixture into the paste.

Form the potato mixture into 16 sausage shapes. With a finger, make a hole in each sausage. Fill with a portion of the pork filling, then close the potato around the filling. Dip each croquette into the egg and water mixture, then roll in the dry breadcrumbs. (The croquettes can be made ahead up to this point.)

Deep fry in hot oil in batches of four for about 1 minute or until golden brown on all sides. Drain on kitchen paper. Tie with chive leaves to decorate and serve hot.

Marinated Mushrooms

Left: *marinated mushrooms.* Right: *herring and apple rolls.*

450g/1 lb small button
  mushrooms
175ml/6fl oz sherry
  vinegar
4 tbsp olive oil
4 tbsp sunflower oil

1 tsp soft brown sugar
3 tbsp finely chopped fresh
  parsley
2 small garlic cloves, finely
  chopped
120g/4oz canned
  pimientoes, drained

illustrated on page 29

Makes about 45-50

Wipe the mushrooms with a damp cloth and pat dry. Combine the vinegar, oils, sugar, parsley and garlic; mix well. Add the mushrooms, toss thoroughly and leave to marinate overnight, stirring occasionally. (The mushrooms may be kept covered, chilled, for up to 2 days.)

Drain the mushrooms thoroughly. Cut the pimientoes into thin strips. Wind a strip decoratively round each mushroom, and skewer both ends through the mushroom with a cocktail stick. Serve.

29

Curd Cheese and Ham Piroshki

225g/8oz plain flour
Salt
90g/3oz butter
60g/2oz lard
1 egg yolk, beaten
Fresh dill sprigs, to garnish

Filling
15g/½ oz butter
60g/2oz brown mushrooms,
  finely chopped
½ small onion, finely
  chopped
1 garlic clove, finely
  chopped
175g/6oz cooked ham,
  finely chopped
120g/4oz Cheese curd
1 tbsp finely chopped fresh
  dill
Salt and black pepper

illustrated on page 27

Makes 12

Combine the flour and salt to taste in a large bowl. Rub in the butter and lard until the mixture resembles breadcrumbs. Sprinkle with 4 tablespoons water, 1 tablespoon at a time, mixing until the dough clings together to form a smooth ball. Wrap and chill for a least 1 hour.

To make the filling, melt the butter in a frying pan and sauté the mushrooms, onion and garlic until softened. Transfer to a bowl and add the ham, curd cheese, dill and seasoning to taste. Mix well and set aside.

Divide the dough in half. Roll out one piece on a lightly floured surface and cut out five or six 8cm/3½ in rounds. Repeat with the remaining dough. Divide the filling among the rounds, moisten the edges and fold over into half-moons to enclose the filling. Crimp the edges of the turnovers with a fork. (The pastries can be made ahead to this point, covered tightly and kept for several hours.)

Preheat the oven to 220°C/425°F/Gas Mark 7. Brush the turnovers with the beaten egg. Place on a baking sheet and bake for 20-25 minutes or until golden brown. Serve immediately, garnished with dill sprigs.

Dilled Salmon Tartlets

150g/5oz plain flour
Salt
120g/4oz butter
1 egg white, lightly beaten

Filling
30g/1oz unsalted butter
175g/6oz spring onions,
  finely chopped
350g/12oz fresh salmon
  fillet, skinned and finely
  chopped
4 egg yolks, beaten
200ml/7fl oz double cream
2 tbsp Angostura bitters
Salt and black pepper
1 tbsp finely chopped fresh
  dill

illustrated on page 31

Makes 16-18

Sift the flour and salt to taste into a bowl and rub in the butter until the mixture resembles breadcrumbs. Add up to 3 tablespoons of water, one at a time, mixing until a smooth ball of dough can be formed. Chill for at least 1 hour.

Preheat the oven to 22°C/425°F/Gas Mark 7. Roll out the dough and cut out 7.5cm/3in rounds. Use to line 16-18 tartlet tins. Prick and brush with the egg white, then bake blind for about 6-8 minutes or until lightly browned. Cool, then turn out of the tins.

To make the filling, melt the butter and sauté half of the spring onions until softened. Stir in the salmon and cook for 4 minutes. In the top of a double boiler, cook the egg yolks, cream, bitters and seasoning to taste, stirring constantly, until the custard has thickened.

Lower the oven heat to 180°C/350°F/Gas Mark 4. Fill each tartlet case with a little salmon mixture and top with the dill. Pour or spoon on the custard. Sprinkle with the remaining spring onion. Bake for 8-10 minutes, until the filling is set. Serve warm. (The tartlets can be made ahead and rewarmed, if necessary.)

Dilled salmon tartlets.

Herring and Apple Rolls

8-10 large marinated
  herring fillets
1 tart red apple, cored and
  quartered

1 small onion, grated
Salt and black pepper
8-10 miniature gherkins,
  halved

illustrated on page 29

Makes 16-20

Drain the herring fillets and cut each lengthways in half. Leaving the skin on the apple, grate it. Mix with the onion. Season to taste. Carefully cut the gherkin halves into fans.

Take a teaspoonful of the apple mixture and place at the thick end of a fillet half. Roll up to the tip and secure with a cocktail stick. Garnish each with a gherkin fan. (These rolls can be made a few hours ahead, covered with cling-film and kept in the refrigerator.)

A Stand-Up Supper

Menu

Leek and Carrot Sticks

Gruyère and Smoked Ham Popovers

Individual Smoked Salmon Roulades

Artichoke-Prawn Cups

Steak Tartare Balls with Mustard Sauce

Strawberry Tartlets

Clockwise from the top: *Leek and Carrot Sticks, Individual Smoked Salmon Roulades, Gruyere and Smoked Ham Popovers, Steak Tartare Balls with Mustard Sauce, Strawberry Tartlets.*

Leek and Carrot Sticks

12-15 small leeks, well
   trimmed top and bottom
30 tiny carrots, trimmed
250ml/8fl oz olive oil
5 tbsp red wine vinegar

1 tsp honey
2 tbsp chopped fresh
   tarragon
Salt and black pepper

illustrated on page 33

Makes about 15

Cut the leeks across into 4cm/1½ in pieces. Plunge into boiling salted water and cook until tender. Remove with a slotted spoon. In the same water, boil the carrots until tender. Drain thoroughly.

Combine the oil, vinegar, honey and tarragon. Add the vegetables and toss thoroughly. Season to taste and leave to marinate for 3-4 hours. (The dish can be made ahead up to this point and kept in the refrigerator.)

Drain the vegetables. Thread them carefully on to small wooden skewers, alternating three leeks and two carrots on each stick. Arrange attractively on a flat dish and serve.

Gruyère and Smoked Ham Popovers

3 size-2 eggs
165g/5½oz plain flour
350ml/12fl oz milk
2 spring onions, finely
   chopped

90g/3oz smoked ham,
   shredded
90g/3oz Gruyère cheese,
   grated

illustrated on page 33

Makes 24

Preheat the oven to 200°C/400°F/Gas Mark 6. Thoroughly grease each cup of two 12-hole bun tins with butter or oil.

In a food processor fitted with a metal blade, or a blender, combine the eggs, flour and milk. Process until completely smooth. Stir in the onions, ham and cheese. Pour the mixture into the prepared cups until they are three-quarters full, and bake for about 15-20 minutes, or until puffed, brown and firm to the touch.

Loosen the popovers with a knife and remove from the tin. Serve piping hot.

Individual Smoked Salmon Roulades

175g/6oz frozen chopped
   spinach, thawed
60g/2oz plain flour
2 eggs
2 tsp sunflower oil
5 tbsp milk
Oil for frying

Filling
150g/5oz cream cheese, at
   room temperature
175g/6oz smoked salmon,
   thinly sliced

illustrated on page 33

Makes 40

Squeeze as much moisture as possible from the spinach and chop it even more finely. In a bowl, mix together the flour, eggs, oil and milk; stir in the spinach.

Lightly oil a pancake pan or griddle and heat it. Pour 2-3 tablespoons of the spinach batter into the pan and swirl to make a pancake about 17.5-20cm/7-8in. in diameter. Cook until lightly browned underneath, then turn over and briefly cook the other side. Tip the pancake out of the pan on to a plate. Repeat with the remaining batter. Allow the pancakes to cool.

Spread each pancake with cream cheese and cover sparingly with smoked salmon slices. Roll up the pancakes and cut across into 2cm/¾in pieces. (These can be made several hours ahead of time if kept covered and chilled.)

Artichoke-Prawn Cups

675-800g/1½-1¾ lb cooked
   peeled prawns
175ml/6fl oz fresh lime
   juice
1 large avocado, finely
   chopped
Salt and black pepper
2 spring onions, finely
   chopped
2 tbsp finely chopped fresh
   coriander leaves

3 tbsp sunflower oil
¼ tsp Tabasco sauce
3x 425g/15oz cans
   artichoke bottoms in brine,
   drained

To garnish
Lime curls
Cherry tomatoes

Makes about 18

In a non-metallic bowl, combine the prawns and lime juice. Cover and chill for 2-4 hours.

Drain off the residue of the lime juice and gently

toss together the prawns, avocado, seasoning, spring onions, coriander, oil and Tabasco sauce.

Cut a thin slice off the base of each artichoke bottom so that it will stand flat. Spoon some of the prawn mixture into each artichoke bottom. Serve soon after making, on a platter garnished with lime curls and cherry tomatoes.

Steak Tartare Balls with Mustard Sauce

675g/1½lb fillet or rump steak	Lemon twists, to garnish
2 onions, finely chopped	**Sauce**
3 tbsp capers, finely chopped	300ml/½ pint mayonnaise
1 tsp Dijon mustard	1 gherkin, finely chopped
Dash of Tabasco sauce	2 spring onions, finely chopped
Salt and black pepper	1 anchovy, very finely chopped
2 small egg yolks	
1 red pepper, seeded and very finely chopped	2 tsp dry mustard
6 tbsp finely chopped fresh parsley	120ml/4fl oz double cream
	½ tsp fresh lemon juice

illustrated on page 33

Makes 20-24

Make the sauce first: combine all the ingredients in a bowl, cover and chill for several hours.

Put the steak through the fine blade of a mincer or ask your butcher to do it for you. (If you do the latter, buy the steak as near as possible to eating it.) In a bowl, mix the steak with the onions, capers, mustard, Tabasco, salt and pepper to taste, and the egg yolks. Combine thoroughly with the hands. Form into small balls; roll half in the finely chopped red pepper and the remainder in the parsley. Serve piled around a bowl containing the sauce, garnished with lemon twists.

Strawberry Tartlets

175g/6oz plain flour	3 tbsp cornflour
Salt	60g/2oz plain flour
90g/3oz cold butter	1 whole egg
30g/1oz lard	1 egg yolk
1 size-4 egg yolk	60g/2oz butter
	Few drops of vanilla essence
Filling	
600ml/1 pint milk	32-36 fresh strawberries
175g/6oz caster sugar	Redcurrant jelly

illustrated on page 33

Makes 16-18

In a bowl, combine the flour and salt to taste. Rub in the butter and lard until the mixture resembles breadcrumbs. Add the egg yolk and enough water (about 1 tablespoon) to bind the dough into a ball. Chill for 1 hour.

Preheat the oven to 180°C/350°F/Gas Mark 4. Roll out the dough and cut out rounds to line 16-18 tartlet tins, each 4-5cm/1½-2in in diameter. Prick, then bake blind for about 10-12 minutes, until golden. Cool and turn out of the tins.

To make the filling: reserve 120ml/4fl oz of the milk and combine the remainder with the sugar in a saucepan. Bring to the boil, then remove from the heat. In a bowl, mix together the cornflour, flour, egg and egg yolk with the reserved milk. Slowly add the egg mixture to the boiled milk, stirring constantly. Return the saucepan to the heat and simmer, stirring, until the custard is thick and smooth. Stir in the butter and vanilla essence until combined; the custard should be glossy. Strain it, cover with dampened greaseproof paper placed directly on the surface and chill. (The tartlets may be made a day ahead to this point.)

To assemble the tartlets, fill the baked pastry cases with the custard and top each with 2 strawberries, sliced. Glaze with the melted jelly.

Spanish Tapas

Fresh sweet almonds are one of the special treats of the Spanish countryside, and spring – when the almond trees are in bloom – is said to be the time to experience rural Spain. The coastal waters of the south and north are both notable for their harvest of molluscs, crustaceans and fish, while garlic and peppers are probably the two vegetable flavours most frequently associated with the Iberian peninsula. Empanadas are old-fashioned peasant pastries, now more associated with the cooking of the New World and the Philippines than with their original home.

Costa Blanca Salad Boats

2 tsp red wine vinegar	175g/6oz rock or Galia
½ tsp dry sherry	melon (peeled weight),
Salt and black pepper	finely diced
2 tbsp olive oil	120g/4oz cooked ham,
120g/4oz small French	chopped
beans, cooked and cut	16 chicory leaves, trimmed
into 1cm/½in lengths	

illustrated on page 37

Makes 16

Whisk together the vinegar and sherry and salt and pepper to taste. Slowly add the oil, whisking, until the dressing is emulsified. Stir in the French beans, melon and ham, and toss gently.

Spoon some of the salad into each of the chicory leaves and arrange decoratively on a platter.

Deep-Fried Prawns

12 medium-sized raw	90-120ml/3-4fl oz beer
prawns, shelled to the tail	1 garlic clove, crushed with
60g/2oz plain flour	the side of a knife
1 tsp baking powder	Lemon twists, to garnish
Salt	Roasted Pepper Dip, to
⅛ tsp cayenne pepper	serve
Groundnut oil for frying	

illustrated on page 39

Makes 12

Pat the prawns dry and remove the black vein down the back, if necessary. In a bowl, mix the flour, baking powder, salt and cayenne. Stir in 1 tablespoon of oil and enough beer to make a coating batter. Leave in a warm place for 30 minutes.

Pour oil to the depth of 2.5cm/1in into a frying pan. Add the garlic, and heat until the garlic browns. Remove it with a slotted spoon. Dip the prawns into the batter, shake off the excess and fry in the hot oil until golden on both sides. Remove with a slotted spoon in batches as cooked and drain on kitchen paper. Serve hot, garnished with lemon twists. It can be accompanied by the Roasted Pepper Dip (recipe on page 40) if preferred.

Clockwise from the top: *vegetable empanadas, Valencian almonds, Costa Blanca salad boats, stuffed mussels Casino.*

Vegetable Empanadas

200g/7oz plain flour
Salt
1 tsp soft light brown sugar
60g/2oz unsalted butter,
    melted
Groundnut oil, for frying
Fresh coriander sprigs, to
    garnish

Filling
120g/4oz potatoes, peeled
    and diced

1 small onion, finely
    chopped
1 fresh green chilli, seeded
    and finely chopped
3 tbsp finely chopped fresh
    coriander leaves
Salt and black pepper
¼ tsp ground cumin
Pinch of dried oregano
60g/2oz raisins

illustrated on page 37

Makes 12-14

In a bowl, combine the flour, salt to taste and sugar. In another bowl, stir the melted butter with 6 table-spoons hot water. Add this to the flour mixture, stirring constantly, until the liquid is absorbed. The mixture will be crumbly. Knead the dough until it will hold shape, then continue to knead on a board until the dough is elastic. Cover and leave to rest overnight.

Blanch the potatoes quickly in boiling water for 2-3 minutes and drain. Sauté the onion in 1 table-spoon oil until it is soft and coloured. Add the potatoes together with the remaining filling ingredients and a further tablespoon oil, and sauté for 4 minutes. Reserve.

Divide the dough in half. Roll out one piece thinly. Cut into 10cm/4in rounds and divide the potato mixture among them. Brush the edges of the dough with water, fold over to make half-moon shapes and crimp the edges with a fork. Repeat the process with the remaining dough and filling.

Deep fry the empanadas, 3 or so at a time, in hot oil for 2 minutes or until golden on both sides. Drain on kitchen paper. Serve hot, garnished with sprigs of coriander.

Lemon-Onion Sardines

2x 120g/4¼oz cans
    sardines in oil, drained
Juice of 1 lemon
6-7 thick slices of brown
    bread
4-5 tbsp prepared lemon
    mayonnaise

2 tsp very finely grated
    lemon zest
1 small red onion, thinly
    sliced and separated into
    rings
Fresh parsley sprigs, to
    garnish

illustrated on page 39

Makes 16-20

Carefully slice the sardines in half lengthways, remove the backbone, and place skin-side down in a shallow dish. Pour over the lemon juice. Cover and chill for 2-3 hours, turning occasionally.

Remove the fish from the juice and leave to drain on kitchen paper. Toast the bread, remove crusts, and cut each slice into 3 fingers. In a small bowl, combine the mayonnaise and the lemon zest. Spread the fingers thinly with the mixture.

Thread each sardine half with 2-3 onion rings, then place on a toast finger. Pipe a little of the remaining flavoured mayonnaise on to each fish toast. Garnish with parsley sprigs.

Stuffed Mussels Casino

24 fresh mussels, well
  scrubbed
120ml/4fl oz white wine
1 celery stalk
4 back bacon rashers, rind
  removed, finely chopped
1 small onion, chopped
1 large garlic clove,
  chopped
1 tbsp olive oil

1 small red pepper, seeded
  and finely chopped
1 small green pepper,
  seeded and finely chopped
1 tsp red wine vinegar
1 tbsp grated Parmesan
  cheese
¼ tsp dried oregano
Salt and black pepper

illustrated on page 37

Makes 24

Place the mussels, white wine, celery and 6fl oz water in a covered saucepan. Bring to the boil and

Left: *deep-fried prawns*. Right: *lemon-onion sardines*.

steam for about 4-5 minutes or until the mussels have opened. It is essential to discard any that remain closed as they are poisonous. Remove from the heat, and allow to cool slightly, then shell the mussels, reserving the meat and half of each shell.

In a frying pan, sauté the bacon, onion and garlic in the oil over medium-low heat until they are all softened and lightly coloured. Add the peppers and cook for a further few minutes, until just tender. Transfer into a bowl and stir in the vinegar, Parmesan, oregano and seasoning to taste. (The mussels and peppers may be prepared to this point and chilled overnight, covered.)

Preheat the oven to 200°C/400°F/Gas Mark 6. Arrange the mussel meat in the half shells, spoon a little of the pepper mixture into each shell, and bake for about 10-12 minutes or until they are heated through. Be careful not to let them dry out too much. Serve immediately.

Peppers with Savoury Filling

2 medium-size red peppers	½ tsp paprika
2 medium-size green peppers	Pinch of cayenne pepper
225g/8oz cream cheese	90g/3oz ready-to-eat dried apricots, chopped
2 tbsp double cream	60g/2oz shelled pistachios, chopped
2 tbsp grated hard Manchego or Parmesan cheese	

illustrated on page 41

Makes about 24

Using a sharp knife, cut off the stalk end of each pepper. Finely chop the flesh of the small piece, discarding the stalk. Reserve. Carefully cut out the ribs and seeds of the peppers without damaging the skins.

In a bowl, combine the cream cheese, cream, grated cheese and spices. Mash well and stir until thoroughly combined. Add the apricots, pistachios and the reserved chopped pepper and mix well. Stuff the peppers with the mixture, cover them tightly and chill for at least 2-3 hours or overnight.

Cut the peppers across into round slices and serve.

Roasted Pepper Dip

200ml/7fl oz bottled or canned roasted red peppers (pimientos), drained and chopped	½ tsp red wine vinegar
	2 tbsp soured cream
	1 tbsp crumbled fresh rosemary leaves
½ tsp Tabasco sauce	

Makes about 250ml/8fl oz

In a food processor or blender, combine the peppers, Tabasco sauce and vinegar and process until smooth. Add the soured cream and process further. Stir in the rosemary, pour into a bowl, and serve.

Albondigas with Garlic Dip

1 slice of bread, crusts removed	Olive oil for frying
2 tbsp malt vinegar	**Dip**
350g/12oz minced pork	4 garlic cloves, finely chopped
6 tbsp finely chopped fresh parsley	Salt and white pepper
2 garlic cloves	2 egg yolks
1 size-2 egg, beaten	250ml/8fl oz olive oil
Salt and black pepper	Juice of ½ lemon

Makes about 30

Make the dip first: in a bowl, crush the garlic pieces as much as possible. Whisk in salt and pepper to taste and the egg yolks. Add the oil in drops, whisking until you have added about 2-3 tablespoons oil. Add the remaining oil in a steady stream, whisking constantly. When the mixture thickens to mayonnaise consistency, add the lemon juice. Cover and chill for at least 2 hours to combine the flavours.

In a large bowl, soak the bread in the vinegar for 10 minutes. Squeeze out as much excess moisture from the bread as possible, then combine the bread with the pork, parsley, garlic and the beaten egg. Add salt and pepper to taste and mix well with the hands until thoroughly blended.

Pick out nut-sized pieces of the mixture and roll into little balls. Heat oil in a frying pan and fry the meatballs in batches until browned on all sides and cooked through. Keep warm in a low oven until all the balls are done.

Serve the garlic dip in a bowl, surrounded by the meatballs. (These can also be served with Roasted Pepper Dip, if preferred.)

Valencian Almonds

Peppers with Savoury Filling

2 tbsp sunflower oil
450g/1 lb blanched
  almonds
100g/3½ oz caster sugar

1 tsp salt
1½ tsp ground cumin
1 tsp crumbled dried red
  chillis

---
illustrated on page 37

Makes about 450g/1lb

Heat the oil in a frying pan until smoking hot. Add the almonds and all but 1 tablespoon of the sugar. Sauté, stirring, until the nuts are golden and the sugar is caramelized.

Shake the almonds from the pan into a bowl containing the salt, cumin, chilli flakes and the remaining sugar. Toss well, then allow to cool to room temperature before serving.

41

Japanese-Style Hors d'Oeuvres

Traditional Japanese preliminaries to the main courses of a meal consist of sashimi – raw fish – and sushi – rice artfully combined with raw fish or vegetables. These specialities require the freshest of seafood, cut with the sharpest of knives, and their preparation usually demands years of training. So we have concentrated on dishes which are easier to prepare but still visually stimulating, such as cooked fish and pickled and salted vegetables, all with a Nipponese accent. Though dessert is not usual in Japan, we have introduced a ginger-spiced cake to round out the flavours.

Yakitori Chicken

3tbsp sake (or dry sherry)	675g/1½ lb skinned and
1 tbsp soy sauce	boned chicken breast, cut
1 tbsp sesame oil	into 2.5x5cm/1x2in pieces
½ tsp grated fresh root	8 spring onions, cut into
ginger	5cm/2in lengths
	2 tbsp sesame seeds

illustrated on page 43

Makes 12

Combine the sake (or dry sherry), soy sauce, sesame oil and grated ginger. Add the chicken and leave to marinate for 8 hours or overnight.

Preheat the grill to moderate.

Drain the chicken, reserving the marinade. Thread the chicken pieces on to small wooden skewers, alternating with the spring onion pieces. Roll the skewers in the sesame seeds and place under the grill. Cook for 10 minutes, turning and basting with the marinade, until the chicken is no longer pink. Serve immediately, before the meat dries.

Easy Spring Rolls

450g/1 lb minced pork	Salt and black pepper
300g/10oz Chinese-style	2½ tbsp cornflour
frozen vegetables, thawed	350g/12oz egg roll squares
and drained	(about 30)
8 spring onions, chopped	Oil for deep frying
60g/2oz fresh bean sprouts	
1 tbsp soy sauce	**To garnish**
2 tbsp sweet sherry	Radishes, trimmed into
1½ tsp grated fresh root	heart shapes
ginger	Carrots, trimmed into heart
2 garlic cloves	shapes

illustrated on page 43

Makes 25-30

In a large bowl, combine the pork with the Chinese-style vegetables, spring onions, bean sprouts, soy sauce, sherry, ginger, garlic and seasoning to taste. In a cup combine the cornflour with 5 tablespoons water to make a smooth paste.

Lay out 8 of the egg roll squares and spoon a little of the filling into the centres. Brush the edges of the squares with the cornflour mixture. Fold the top of each egg square over and tuck in the sides. Roll up securely. Repeat with the remaining egg squares and filling. (The rolls can be made to this stage, covered tightly and chilled for up to 1 day.)

Heat oil until very hot and deep fry the rolls, in batches, for about 4 minutes, or until golden. Drain on kitchen paper and keep warm. Serve with a bowl of Chilli Dipping Sauce and garnish with the radish and carrot hearts.

Clockwise from the top: *yakitori chicken, easy spring rolls, lemon ginger dipping sauce, miniature fish cakes.*

Grilled Tuna Sushi

450g/1 lb tuna fillet(s)
4 tbsp dry sherry
120ml/4fl oz rice vinegar
3 tbsp light soy sauce
1 tsp salt
1 tsp caster sugar

450g/1 lb Japanese
  glutinous short-grain rice
2 tsp wasabi paste
Nori, cut into strips
Radishes, halved, to
  garnish

illustrated on page 45

Makes 25–30

Rinse and dry the tuna fillet(s) and cut the fish into 2.5 x 7.5cm/1 x 3in strips.

In a saucepan, mix together the sherry, vinegar, soy sauce, salt and sugar. Bring to the boil. Take off the heat and pour half of the liquid into a large bowl; reserve the remainder in the saucepan.

Put the rice and 600ml/1 pint water in another saucepan and bring to the boil. Cover and cook over low heat for 15 minutes. Remove from the heat and leave, covered, for a further 10 minutes. Turn the rice into the saucepan of reserved liquid and toss to combine thoroughly. Leave to cool to room temperature for several hours.

When the liquid in the bowl has cooled, add the fish strips and marinate for 30 minutes. Preheat the grill to high and cook the fish, turning once or twice, for about 4-5 minutes, or until just done.

Using dampened hands, shape the rice into 25 or more sausage shapes. Brush each rice sausage with a little wasabi and gently press a tuna strip into the rice. Wind a moistened strip of nori around each sushi. Keep the sushi covered with a damp cloth until ready to serve. Garnish with radish halves.

Miniature Fish Cakes

350g/12oz cod fillet
450g/1 lb mashed potatoes
2 eggs
2 tbsp chopped fresh parsley
Salt and black pepper
2 tsp lemon juice

60g/2oz mooli or radish,
  shredded
1 tsp wasabi paste
2 tbsp plain flour
90g/3oz dry breadcrumbs
Oil
Fresh chives, to garnish

illustrated on page 43

Makes 20-24

Preheat the oven to 180°C/350°F/Gas Mark 4. Bake the cod fillets until just done, about 10 minutes. Flake the cod into a bowl, discarding any skin, and mix with the potatoes, 1 egg, the parsley, seasoning to taste, lemon juice, shredded mooli or radish and wasabi paste.

Spread the flour and breadcrumbs on separate plates, and beat the remaining egg in a fairly shallow dish.

Divide the cod mixture into small balls and shape each into a little round cake. Coat the cakes in flour, then dip into the egg and, finally, dredge thoroughly in the breadcrumbs.

In a frying pan, heat enough oil to come halfway up the cakes. Fry the cakes in two batches, for 2-3 minutes on each side, until crisp and golden. Drain on kitchen paper and keep warm until serving, with Lemon Ginger Dipping Sauce and/or Chilli Dipping Sauce. Garnish with the chives.

Teriyaki Beef Cakes

675g/1½ lb lean minced beef	ginger
	1 tbsp dry sherry
3 tbsp finely chopped spring onion	4 tsp soy sauce
	Salt and black pepper
2 garlic cloves, crushed	15g/½ oz butter
2 tsp shredded fresh root	Onion brushes, to garnish

Makes 24

Mix together the beef, spring onion, garlic, ginger, sherry, 3tsp soy sauce, and salt and pepper to taste in a bowl. Shape into small round cakes.

Heat the butter in a frying pan with the remaining soy sauce and fry the cakes for about 5 minutes, turning once, until crisp and brown on the outside and still pink inside. Garnish with onion brushes and serve immediately, with the Chilli Dipping Sauce if wished.

Left: *grilled tuna sushi.* Right: *pickled baby vegetables.*

Lemon Ginger Dipping Sauce

1 tbsp cornflour	1 tbsp soft brown sugar
4 tbsp fresh lemon juice	1 tsp grated fresh root
175-250ml/6-8fl oz chicken or fish stock	ginger
1 tbsp honey	1 tsp finely chopped fresh chives

---

illustrated on page 43

Makes about 250ml/8fl oz

In a saucepan, stir together the cornflour and lemon juice. Over low heat, slowly stir in the stock followed by the honey, sugar, and ginger. Continue stirring until the sauce thickens. Add more stock if the sauce is too thick. Whisk in the chives and pour into a serving bowl. (This can be made ahead of time and allowed to cool.)

East-West Ginger Roll

90g/3oz plain flour
¾ tsp baking powder
Salt
2 tsp ground ginger
3 eggs
120g/4oz caster sugar
1 tsp vanilla essence
Icing sugar

Filling
450ml/¾ pint double cream
320g/11½ oz marmalade
1 tbsp preserved stem
   ginger, finely chopped

To decorate
Crystallized ginger
Candied angelica, cut into
   fans

illustrated on page 47

Makes 10 slices

Preheat the oven to 200°C/400°F/Gas Mark 6. Line a 24 x 34cm/ 9½ x 13½ in Swiss roll tin with buttered greaseproof paper. In a large bowl, combine the flour, baking powder, salt to taste and ginger. In another bowl, beat the eggs until yellow and fluffy. Gradually beat in the caster sugar until the mixture is thick and light. Beat in the vanilla, then carefully fold into the prepared tin and spread so that it evenly reaches all the corners.

Bake for about 20 minutes, or until the cake springs back when lightly pressed, but is not brown. Remove from the oven and cool in the tin for several minutes. Spread out a tea towel on the work surface and sprinkle with sifted icing sugar. Turn the cake on to the towel and peel off the lining paper. Roll up the cake from a short end, using the towel to help. Cool completely.

To make the filling, whip the cream until stiff. Set aside a little of the whipped cream, and stir the marmalade and chopped stem ginger into the remainder.

Unroll the cake and spread the marmalade cream over it, right to the edges. Roll up again loosely and set on a serving dish. Pipe the reserved cream on the rolled cake and decorate with crystallized ginger and angelica fans.

Pickled Baby Vegetables

225g/8oz cauliflower, cut
   into small florets
225g/8oz carrots, cut into
   thin 7.5cm/3in sticks
225g/8oz baby courgettes,
   cut into 7.5cm/3in sticks
1 red pepper, seeded and cut
   into thin sticks
175g/6oz baby sweetcorn

250ml/8fl oz white wine
   vinegar
60g/2oz caster sugar
1 tsp salt
1 tsp mustard seeds
1 tsp coriander seeds
1 tsp black peppercorns
½ tsp juniper berries,
   crushed

illustrated on page 45

Makes about 800g/1¾ lb

Drop the five vegetables into boiling water, return to the boil, then drain immediately. Refresh under running cold water and drain again.

In a large non-metallic bowl, combine the vinegar, sugar, salt and spices, and stir until the sugar dissolves. Add the drained vegetables. Cover and chill for 2 days, tossing the vegetables occasionally.

Drain the vegetables thoroughly and arrange attractively so that they can be handled easily with the fingers.

East-West ginger roll.

Toasted Pumpkin Seeds

Seeds from a 1.35kg/3 lb
piece of pumpkin

25g/¾oz butter
Salt

Makes about 90g/3oz

Clean the seeds of any membrane left over from
the pumpkin. Spread the seeds on kitchen paper to
dry at room temperature for 2 days or in an airing
cupboard for 1 day.

Remove the seeds from the paper and sauté them
in the melted butter over medium heat for about 2
minutes or until golden. Transfer to kitchen paper
to drain. Season to taste with salt, cool and store in
an airtight container.

Chilli Dipping Sauce

1 tbsp bottled oriental fish
  sauce
4 anchovy fillets
3 tbsp fresh lime juice
6 garlic cloves

1 tbsp light soy sauce
1 tsp caster sugar
2 fresh red or green chillis,
  seeded and finely chopped

Makes about 150ml/¼ pint

Put all the ingredients into a food processor or
blender and process until you have a smooth paste.
Thin slightly with boiling water, if necessary. Try
with the spring rolls or the fish/beef cakes.

Tea-Time Titbits

Menu

Sweet Potato Cheese Scones

Cinnamon Spirals

Mango Waldorf Chicken Sandwiches

Fruitcake Biscuits

Apricot and Raspberry Tartlets

Minted Cucumber Sandwiches

Clockwise from the top: cinnamon spirals, sweet potato cheese scones, apricot and raspberry tartlets, fruitcake biscuits, mango Waldorf chicken sandwiches.

Sweet Potato Cheese Scones

1 medium-size sweet potato	30g/1oz unsalted butter,
225g/8oz self-rising flour	softened
2 tsp caster sugar	2 tbsp dry sherry
Salt	½ tsp Worcester sauce
120-150ml/4-5fl oz milk	½ tsp prepared English
	mustard
Spread	1 tbsp milk
225g/8oz Cheddar cheese	1 tbsp chopped spring
60g/2oz Danish blue cheese	onions

illustrated on page 49

Makes about 22-24

Make the cheese spread 2-3 days ahead of time to let the flavours mingle. In the bowl of a food processor, grate the cheeses. Add all the other ingredients for the spread, and process until thoroughly combined and smooth. Scrape into a bowl, cover and chill. (Alternatively, grate the cheeses by hand, mash together with the butter, and combine with all the other ingredients, one after another, beating by hand after each addition.

Preheat the oven to 200°C/400°F/Gas Mark 6. Grease the skin of the sweet potato, pierce in a few places with a fork and bake for 45 minutes to 1 hour or until soft. Cool slightly, then peel and mash.

Sift the flour, sugar and salt to taste into a bowl. Stir in 225g/8oz of the mashed sweet potato and 120ml/4fl oz of the milk. Work to a soft dough ; if it is too stiff, then add the remaining milk a little at a time. Turn the dough on to a floured surface and knead briefly until smooth. Press out with the hands until it is 1-2 cm/½-¾in thick, then cut 4-5cm/1½-2in rounds.

Keep the oven at 200°C/400°F/Gas Mark 6. Place the sweet potato scones on a greased baking tray, brush with a little milk, and bake for about 15 minutes or until browned. Remove from the tray and cool slightly on a wire rack.

Split the scones while still warm, stuff with the cheese spread and serve immediately or serve halved and spread with the cheese mixture.

Cinnamon Spirals

10 large slices of white	60g/2oz sugar
bread, crusts removed	2 tsp ground cinnamon
60-90g/3oz butter, melted	

illustrated on page 49

Makes 20

Place the slices of bread between two sheets of greaseproof paper and, with a rolling pin, roll as flat and thin as possible without tearing.

Preheat the oven to 180°C/350°F/Gas Mark 4. Brush both sides of the bread slices with the melted butter. Mix together the sugar and cinnamon in a bowl, then evenly dust one side of each slice of bread with some of the mixture. Roll up the slices from a long side, cinnamon-side in. Trim the top and bottom of the roll on the diagonal, and cut diagonally across the centre of each roll. Secure each piece with a wooden cocktail stick.

Place the rolls on a baking sheet and bake for about 15-20 minutes, or until golden. Remove the sticks and serve.

Mango Waldorf Chicken Sandwiches

3 small red apples, cored	450g/1 lb cooked white
and finely chopped	chicken meat, shredded
3 celery stalks, finely	Salt and black pepper
chopped	2 tsp Dijon mustard
60g/2oz shelled pecan	12 slices of white or brown
nuts, chopped	bread
250ml/8fl oz mayonnaise	6 lettuce leaves, halved
150ml/¼ pint soured	
cream	**To Garnish**
4 tbsp mango chutney	12 large pecan nut halves
	Fresh parsley sprigs

illustrated on page 49

Makes 12

In a bowl, mix the apples, celery and chopped pecans. Add 150ml/¼ pint of the mayonnaise, the soured cream and mango chutney, and fold together. In another bowl, toss the shredded chicken with salt and pepper to taste.

In a small bowl, whisk together the remaining mayonnaise and the mustard. With a 7.5cm/3 inch round biscuit cutter, cut rounds from the bread slices. Spread each round generously with the mustard mayonnaise, top with half a lettuce leaf and divide the shredded chicken among them. Pile small mounds of the apple and celery mixture on top, and garnish each with a pecan nut half and sprig of parsley. (These can be made ahead, covered tightly and chilled for 2-3 hours.)

Fruitcake Biscuits

175g/6oz plain flour	*120g/4oz shelled walnuts, chopped*
¼ tsp bicarbonate of soda	*120g/4oz shelled brazil nuts, chopped*
Salt	
½ tsp ground cinnamon	*120g/4oz blanched almonds, chopped*
¼ tsp ground cloves	
60g/2oz butter, softened	*60g/2oz raisins*
120g/4oz soft light brown sugar	*175g/6oz stoned dates, chopped*
2 eggs	*90g/3oz chopped candied peel*
175-250ml/6-8fl oz medium or sweet sherry	*175g/6oz glacé cherries, quartered*
1 tsp vanilla essence	

illustrated on page 49

Makes about 60

Preheat the oven to 150°C/300°F/Gas Mark 2. In a bowl combine the flour, soda, salt to taste, cinnamon and cloves. In a larger bowl use an electric mixer to cream the butter sugar, then add the eggs and beat well. Beat in half the sherry, then add half the flour mixture and combine well. Add the rest of the sherry, the vanilla, and then the rest of the flour, beating well after each. Fold in the nuts and fruit by hand, combining well.

Drop heaped spoonfuls of the mixture on to greased baking trays, leaving space between the heaps. Bake the biscuits in four batches for 25-30 minutes. Allow to cool on the trays before removing the biscuits with a fish slice. Keep in an airtight tin.

Apricot and Raspberry Tartlets

175g/6oz plain flour	**Filling**
3 tbsp icing sugar	*120g/4oz prepared almond paste*
120g/4oz firm butter	
1 egg yolk	*90g/3oz butter, softened*
½ tsp almond essence	*1 egg white*
	30g/1oz icing sugar, sifted
	1 tbsp Kirsch or brandy
	4 tbsp apricot jam
	4 tbsp raspberry jam

illustrated on page 49

Makes 24

First make the pastry cases: in a bowl, combine the flour and sugar. Rub in the butter until the mixture resembles breadcrumbs. In another bowl, beat together the egg yolk, almond essence and 1 tablespoon water. Add to the dry mixture and combine to make a smooth, sticky dough.

Preheat the oven to 180°C/350°F/Gas Mark 4. Pinch off small pieces of the dough and press into 4-5cm/1½-2in tartlet tins.

Beat the almond paste with the butter, egg white, sugar and spirit until smooth. Fill each pastry case with the almond paste mixture, about half full. Bake for 25 minutes, or until the pastry is golden and the filling firm.

Remove the tartlets from the oven. Heat the jams in two separate pans. (You may want to chop the apricots into small pieces before heating the jam.) Drop a teaspoonful of apricot jam on to half of the tartlets and a teaspoonful of the raspberry jam on to the others.

Cool the tartlets before removing from the tins and serving. (These may be made up to 3 days ahead and kept in an airtight tin.)

Minted Cucumber Sandwiches

1 cucumber	**Spread**
Salt	*2 large egg yolks*
12 thin slices of white or brown bread, crusts removed	*½ tsp Dijon mustard*
	2 tbsp fresh lemon juice
	60g/2oz fresh mint leaves
Finely chopped fresh mint	*250ml/8fl oz sunflower oil*
	Salt and black pepper

Makes 24

Thinly slice the cucumber. Layer with salt, weight it and leave to drain for 3-4 minutes. Process the egg yolks, mustard, lemon juice and mint until thoroughly combined. With the motor running, gradually add the oil in a slow stream and process until the mixture is emulsified into a mayonnaise. Season and chill. Drain off the cucumber slices, rinse, pat dry, cover and chill. Make six sandwiches filled with thickly spread mint mayonnaise and cucumber and cut each into quarters.

Scandinavian Smörgäsbord

All of the Scandinavian countries have a version of this groaning table, usually containing open-faced sandwiches in Denmark (the 'buttered bread' of the Danish Smorresbrød). It is usually rich in herring and other native fish presented in a variety of ways, as well as eggs, hot meat casseroles and vegetable salads. Here we combine some of the traditional flavours associated with Northern climes: salmon and smoked fish, dill, sweet/sour red berries, beetroot and potatoes, and eggs in two styles. Pass round the aquavit and cold beer or sparkling fruit drinks.

Scrambled Egg Avocados

10 eggs	*2 celery stalks, finely*
25g/3/4oz butter	*chopped*
4 tbsp mayonnaise	*12 miniature avocados,*
4 tbsp soured cream	*halved, seeded if necessary,*
1 tbsp Dijon mustard	*skinned and rubbed with*
Salt and black pepper	*lemon juice*
2 tsp curry powder	*Fresh parsley sprigs, to*
1 small red onion, finely	*garnish*
chopped	

Makes 24

Beat the eggs lightly. Melt the butter in a saucepan over low heat and stir in the eggs. Gently scramble until you have creamy curds. Remove from the heat and allow to cool slightly, then mix in the mayonnaise, soured cream, mustard, seasoning to taste, curry powder, and finely chopped onion and celery. (This can be made 1 day ahead and kept in the refrigerator.)

Prepare the avocados as near to the time of serving as possible, and rub them all over with lemon juice to prevent discolouration. Pile the egg mixture on to the avocado halves and garnish decoratively with parsley sprigs.

Sweet & Sour Pink Potatoes

6 smallish (but not new)	*2 tsp reserved beetroot juice*
potatoes	*1 tbsp Demerara sugar*
½ red onion, finely chopped	*2 tsp Dijon mustard*
1 gherkin, finely chopped	*Small chunks of herring in*
3 small pickled beetroot,	*soured cream*
finely chopped	*Fresh parsley, to garnish*
3 tbsp soured cream	

illustrated on page 53

Makes 12

Preheat the oven to 200°C/400°F/Gas Mark 6. Grease the potato skins, then bake the potatoes for 30 minutes or until soft. Remove and allow to cool slightly, for easier handling.

Cut the potatoes in half and scoop the flesh carefully into a bowl, leaving the skin intact. Mash the potato and gently mix in the remaining ingredients, except the herring. Pile the filling into the reserved potato skin shells. (The potatoes may be prepared ahead to this point and chilled for up to 1 day. Return to room temperature before serving.)

Top each stuffed potato with one or two small chunks of herring, and garnish with the parsley.

Clockwise from the top: *sweet & sour pink potatoes, smoked haddock croquettes with Tartare sauce, open-faced gravadlax sandwiches, turkey puffs with cranberry relish.*

Smoked Haddock Croquettes with Tartare Sauce

350g/12oz smoked haddock	1 egg yolk
2 eggs	3 tbsp fresh lemon juice
4 tbsp plain flour	2 tbsp Dijon mustard
4 tbsp instant potato flakes	½ tsp cayenne pepper
1 onion, grated	Salt
Black pepper	350ml/12fl oz sunflower oil
1 heaped tsp baking powder	5 spring onions, finely chopped
1 tbsp finely chopped fresh tarragon	2 tbsp finely chopped sweet/sour gherkin
Oil for deep frying	1 tbsp capers
Fresh tarragon leaves, to garnish	1 tsp Worcestershire sauce
	½ tsp soy sauce
Sauce	1 tbsp Tabasco sauce
1 whole egg	2 tbsp finely chopped fresh parsley

illustrated on page 53

Makes 24

Make the sauce first. In a food processor or blender, combine the whole egg and egg yolk, the lemon juice, mustard, cayenne and salt to taste. Mix until smooth. With the motor running, add the oil in a thin stream and blend until thickened into a mayonnaise. Add the remaining ingredients and process in short bursts until thoroughly combined. Cover and chill for at least 2 hours. (This makes enough sauce to reserve some for future use. Keep, covered and chilled, for up to 2 weeks.)

Simmer the smoked haddock in water to cover until it flakes. Drain thoroughly, remove all skin and bones and flake into a bowl. Mix in the eggs and stir in the flour. When well combined, stir in the potato flakes, onion, pepper to taste, the baking powder and chopped tarragon. Form the mixture into small sausage shapes. (These may be made 1 day ahead and chilled, covered.)

Drop the croquettes into the hot oil in batches and deep fry for 3-4 minutes until golden brown. Remove as done with a slotted spoon and drain on kitchen paper. Serve the croquettes hot, garnished with tarragon leaves, surrounding a bowl of the tartare sauce.

Open-Faced Gravadlax Sandwiches

1.1-1.3kg/2½ -3lb salmon tail, filleted, but skin left on	Finely chopped fresh dill
	Lemon slices dipped in parsley, to garnish
90g/3oz fresh dill or fennel leaves, chopped	
½ tsp coarse sea salt	**Sauce**
1 tbsp freshly ground black pepper	4-5 tbsp Dijon mustard
4 tbsp olive oil	1 tsp dry mustard
4 tbsp sunflower oil	3 tbsp caster sugar
10 thin slices of dark rye or pumpernickel bread	2 tbsp white wine vinegar
	4 ½ tbsp sunflower oil

illustrated on page 53

Makes 40

Wash the two salmon fillets and pat dry. Inspect for small bones and remove them with tweezers. Place one fillet, skin-side down, in a shallow glass or glazed china dish. Sprinkle the exposed flesh with the dill leaves, salt and pepper. Mix the two oils together and pour over the fish. Place the other fillet, skin-side up, on top. Cover the dish tightly and place a weight (such as a book or heavy plate) on top. Chill for 3 days, turning the sandwiched fillets at least twice a day and spooning over the juices.

To make the sauce, mix together the mustards, sugar and vinegar, until the sugar has dissolved. Add the oil in drops, whisking, and then in a thin stream, until the sauce has thickened. Chill until ready to use.

To make the sandwiches: drain the salmon and thinly slice it against the grain, detaching it from the skin. Spread the sauce on the bread and cover with the salmon slices. Cut each sandwich into quarters and top each piece with a little chopped dill. Garnish with lemon slices.

Left: *orange eggs.*
Right: *fancy Swedish meetballs with redcurrant sauce.*

Lemon Cheese Pancakes

100g/ 3½ oz plain flour	**Filling**
2 tbsp caster sugar	6 tbsp caster sugar
Salt	½ tsp grated lemon zest
2 eggs, lightly beaten	2 tbsp fresh lemon juice
250ml/8fl oz milk	3 egg yolks
½ tsp vanilla essence	450g/1 lb cottage cheese
Butter for frying	½ tsp vanilla essence
Icing sugar	
Ground cinnamon	

Makes 12

Make the filling first: combine the sugar, lemon zest and juice and egg yolks in a bowl and mix them thoroughly together. Slowly whisk in the cottage cheese and then the vanilla essence. This can then be set aside while you make the pancakes, or cover and chill for up to 1 day ahead. (Bring to room temperature before using.)

Sift the flour, sugar and salt to taste into a large bowl. In another bowl, mix together the eggs, milk and vanilla essence. Make a well in the centre of the dry mixture and pour in the egg mixture. Whisk to make a thin, smooth batter.

Heat a griddle or non-stick frying pan until medium-hot. Grease with butter and pour in 1-1½ tablespoons of the batter, swirling it around to make a small pancake about 12.5-15cm/5-6in in diameter. Cook until lightly browned, then flip over and briefly cook the other side. Remove from the griddle and keep warm in a low oven. Re-butter the griddle and make 11 more pancakes in the same way. Stir the batter between pancakes to keep it from thickening.

Place some of the filling in the centre of each small pancake; tuck in the sides and roll up. Dust the tops with sifted icing sugar and cinnamon, arrange in an attractive pile and serve.

If desired, blueberries or redcurrants can be added to the cottage cheese filling.

Fancy Swedish Meatballs with Redcurrant Sauce

90g/3oz fresh breadcrumbs	**Sauce**
175ml/6fl oz soda water	4 tbsp redcurrant jelly
45g/1½ oz butter	2 tsp cornflour
1 onion, finely chopped	2 tsp red wine vinegar
350g/12oz minced beef	4 tbsp dry red wine
350g/12oz minced veal	4 tbsp port
175g/6oz minced pork	Juice of ½ orange
Salt and black pepper	1 tsp dry mustard
1 egg, beaten	1 tsp grated orange zest
Fresh coriander leaves, to garnish	½ tsp ground ginger

illustrated on page 55

Makes 35-40

Make the sauce first: in a saucepan, melt the red-currant jelly. Stir in the cornflour and continue to cook until thickened. Take off the heat, stir in the other sauce ingredients, and pour into an attractive bowl. Set aside to come to room temperature. (The sauce may be made up to 3 days ahead and chilled. Bring to room temperature before serving.)

In a large bowl, combine the breadcrumbs and soda, and soak for a few minutes. Heat 15g/½ oz of the butter in a frying pan and sauté the onion until just coloured. Add to the breadcrumbs with the three meats, seasoning to taste, and the egg. Mix with the hands until thoroughly combined and stiffened. Form the mixture into small balls. (The meatballs may be made up to 1 day ahead and kept covered and chilled.)

Melt the remaining butter in the frying pan and sauté the meatballs in batches until they are browned. Pierce with cocktail sticks and serve with the redcurrant sauce, garnished with coriander.

Creamy Prawn Shells

16 frozen medium-sized vol-au-vent cases	Salt and black pepper
175g/6oz peeled cooked prawns, thawed if frozen and well drained	200ml/7fl oz milk
	2 egg yolks
	1 tbsp tomato ketchup
45g/1½ oz butter	120ml/4fl oz double cream
60g/2oz plain flour	90g/3oz frozen peas, thawed
½ tsp chopped fresh chives	Fresh chives, to garnish
½ tsp cayenne pepper	

illustrated on page 57

Makes 16

Bake the frozen vol-au-vents as directed on the packet. Set aside to cool slightly while making the filling.

Reserve 16 prawns for the garnish; chop the remainder. Melt the butter in a saucepan and blend in the flour followed by the chives, cayenne, and salt and pepper to taste. Cook for about 4 minutes, stirring constantly. Remove from the heat and slowly whisk in the milk. Return the saucepan to the heat and cook, stirring constantly, until the sauce has thickened.

In a bowl, whisk together the egg yolks and ketchup. Add a tablespoon of the hot sauce to the egg mixture, stirring. Reduce the heat to very low, then slowly add the egg mixture to the remaining sauce in the pan, stirring. When the sauce begins to thicken, remove from the heat and whisk in the cream. Add the chopped prawns and peas. The mixture should be quite thick.

Shortly before they are to be served, spoon a little of the prawn mixture into each vol-au-vent. Garnish with the reserved prawns and chopped chives. Serve warm.

Orange Eggs

175ml/6fl oz unsweetened orange juice	10 cardamom pods
	Pinch of dill seeds
175ml/6fl oz white wine vinegar	6 hard-boiled eggs, shelled
	12 canned mandarin orange segments
1 onion, sliced	24 capers, drained
2 tbsp sugar	6 small canned anchovies, rinsed, drained and halved
½ tsp salt	
8 black peppercorns, crushed	
8 juniper berries, crushed	Endive leaves, to garnish
1x 5cm/2in cinnamon stick	

illustrated on page 55

Makes 12

Combine all the ingredients, except the eggs, orange segments, capers, anchovies and endive leaves, in a saucepan. Bring to the boil, then reduce the heat and simmer for 5 minutes.

Place the eggs in a large bowl. Pour over the hot marinade and cover tightly. Chill for 8 hours or overnight, turning the eggs occasionally.

Remove the eggs and discard the marinade. Slice each egg in half, and garnish the top of each half with an orange segment and two capers nestled in a curled anchovy. Arrange on a platter and garnish with the endive leaves.

Turkey Puffs with Cranberry Relish

250ml/8fl oz mayonnaise
1 tsp finely chopped fresh dill
4 spring onions, finely chopped
8 slices of wholemeal bread, crusts removed, toasted
4 sour dill gherkins, sliced
450g/1 lb cooked turkey breast meat, sliced
4 egg whites
Salt and black pepper
120g/4oz Havarti or Samsoe cheese, grated
Paprika

Relish
120g/4oz fresh or frozen cranberries, washed, dried and chopped
2 dessert apples, cored and finely chopped
½ tsp lemon juice
1 tbsp honey
2 spring onions, finely chopped
3 tbsp raisins, finely chopped
Salt

Creamy prawn shells.

illustrated on page 53

Makes 16

Make the relish first. In a small bowl, combine all the ingredients. Cover and chill for at least 1 hour.

In a bowl, beat together the mayonnaise, dill and spring onions. Spread the toast slices with the mayonnaise mixture, divide the gherkin slices among them, and top with the turkey slices. Cut the turkey toasts in half diagonally.

Preheat the grill to high.

Whisk the egg whites until stiff, and fold in salt and pepper to taste, the cheese and ½ teaspoon of paprika. Top the toast triangles with the cheese mixture and grill for about 1 minute or until puffed and golden. (Do this in two batches if necessary.)

Sprinkle the tops with a little more paprika and serve hot. Spoon a little of the cranberry relish on to each toast before eating.

English Nibbles

British cooking has long struggled against a reputation for dullness and stodginess. But finally a fresh respect for the classics of England, Scotland and Wales – mature hard cheese, minced and potted meats, fresh seafood and quality green vegetables – with accents provided by cider, beer, whisky and home-made chutneys – has won a new generation of converts. These mouthfuls provide some of the delicious examples of the savoury diversity that can be found in Britain.

Open-Faced Oyster Sandwiches

4 mini baguettes
90g/3oz butter, melted
10 streaky bacon rashers,
   rind removed, chopped
2x 275g/10oz jars oysters
   in brine, drained and
   chopped

175g/6oz Wensleydale
   cheese, grated
Watercress sprigs, to
   garnish

Makes 16

Preheat the oven to 190°C/375°F/Gas Mark 5. Trim off the ends of the baguettes and cut each baguette across into 4 slices. Brush each slice with melted butter and bake in the oven for 10 minutes or until toasted and golden. Remove and cool.

In a frying pan, fry the bacon until almost crisp. Lift out the bacon pieces with a slotted spoon and drain on kitchen paper. Add the oysters to the pan and cook, stirring until curling, for about 2-3 minutes. Drain the oysters carefully on kitchen paper.

Combine the bacon and oysters. (The topping may be made ahead to this point and chilled for up to 2 days.) Divide the mixture between the 16 toast slices. Top with the grated cheese. Return to the oven and bake until the cheese has melted, about 4 minutes. Serve garnished with watercress sprigs.

Curried Mustard Sauce

175ml/6fl oz chilled
   whipping cream, softly
   whipped

1 tsp curry powder
2 tsp prepared horseradish
2 tbsp Dijon mustard

Makes about 175ml/6fl oz

Mix together all the ingredients until well combined. Serve the sauce in a decorative bowl with the Farmhouse Sausage Rolls or the Miniature Scotch Eggs.

Clockwise from the top: *farmhouse sausage rolls, Cheddar-hazelnut crackers, chestnut-stuffed Brussels, miniature Scotch eggs.*

58

Whisky-Scented Bread Pudding

450g/1 lb stale white
  bread, crusts removed
750ml/1¼ pints milk
4 eggs
225g/8oz demerara sugar
90g/3oz butter, melted
1 tbsp whisky

1½ tbsp vanilla essence
120g/4oz raisins
60g/2oz chopped candied
  peel
Grated zest of 1 small
  orange
Icing sugar

---

illustrated on page 61

Makes 15-20 squares

Tear the bread into pieces and put into a large bowl. Pour over the milk and allow to soak for at least 1 hour.

Preheat the oven to 160°C/325°F/Gas Mark 3. Butter a 20 x 25cm/8 x 10in baking tin generously.

In another bowl, beat the eggs with the sugar until pale and fluffy. Beat in the butter, whisky and vanilla essence. Stir this into the bread mixture, followed by the raisins, candied peel and orange zest. Combine thoroughly.

Pour the mixture into the prepared baking tin, carefully levelling the surface. Bake in the middle of the oven until set and browned on top for about 1½ hours. Allow to cool for 15-20 minutes, then dust with sifted icing sugar. Cut into 15-20 squares, put into paper cake cases and serve warm or at room temperature.

Chestnut-Stuffed Brussels

150g/5oz canned
  unsweetened chestnut
  purée
60g/2oz cream cheese
1 tsp lemon juice
Salt and black pepper

30 Brussels sprouts,
  trimmed
6 ready-to-eat stoned
  prunes, each cut into
  5 strips

---

illustrated on page 59

Makes 30

Combine the chestnut purée, cream cheese and lemon juice in a bowl; season to taste.

Cook the Brussels sprouts in boiling salted water until just tender but still crisp.

Drain thoroughly, refresh under cold water, and leave to cool. With a sharp knife, cut into the bottom of each sprout and take out some of the core. Discard these and trim the rounded tops so that they stand up. Pipe the purée mixture into the holes with a star tube and garnish the top with a slice of prune. (These can be made ahead and chilled for 2-3 hours.)

Farmhouse Sausage Rolls

225g/8oz plain flour
120g/4oz cold unsalted
  butter
60g/2oz curd cheese
3-4 tbsp milk
2 tbsp Dijon mustard

450g/1 lb cooked herb
  sausages, skinned
1 egg, beaten

To Garnish
Tomato quarters
Fresh parsley sprigs

---

illustrated on page 59

Makes about 30

Put the flour in a mixing bowl and rub in the butter until the mixture resembles coarse crumbs. Thin the curd cheese with 2-3 tablespoons of the milk and stir into the flour mixture; add more milk, if necessary, to form a stiff dough.

Preheat the oven to 200°C/400°F/Gas Mark 6. Roll out the dough on a floured surface to an oblong about 40 x 25cm/16 x 10in. Cut in half lengthways to make two strips. Spread each strip with mustard.

Lay the skinned sausages end to end down the centre of each strip. Brush the edges of the strips with a little beaten egg, then fold the dough over the sausages and press the edges together firmly to seal. Brush all over with beaten egg and cut across into 2.5cm/1in lengths. Cut a slit in the top of each sausage roll.

Place on a greased baking sheet and bake for 20-25 minutes or until golden. Cool. Serve the sausages rolls with the Curried Mustard Sauce (recipe on p. 58), if desired. Garnish with tomato quarters and parsley.

Stilton-Walnut Grapes

Left: *Stilton-walnut grapes.*
Right: *whisky-scented bread pudding.*

120g/4oz Stilton cheese,
  crumbled
120g/4oz cream cheese
35 seedless green grapes

150g/5oz shelled walnuts,
  toasted and very finely
  chopped
4 tsp finely chopped fresh
  parsley

illustrated on page 61

Makes 35

In a bowl, cream together the Stilton and the cream cheese, by hand or with an electric mixer, until smooth. Take a small amount of the cheese mixture and roll it around a grape. Repeat with the remaining grapes until all are covered.

In another bowl, combine the walnuts and parsley. Roll the cheese balls in the mixture one at a time, until they are liberally coated. Arrange the cheese balls attractively and serve. (These may be made ahead and chilled, covered, for 2-3 hours.)

Cheddar-Hazelnut Crackers

120g/4oz mature Cheddar
  cheese, grated
90g/3oz cold unsalted
  butter
120g/4oz plain flour

60g/2oz shelled hazelnuts,
  finely chopped
1 tbsp garlic purée
Salt and white pepper

illustrated on page 59

Makes about 40-45

In a food processor fitted with the metal blade, blend together the Cheddar cheese, butter, flour, hazelnuts, garlic purée, and salt and pepper to taste. Process until a ball of dough is formed. Divide the dough in half and form each piece into a log about 15cm/6in long, and 4cm/1½in wide. Wrap and chill for 2 hours, or until firm enough to slice.

Preheat the oven to 200°C/400°F/Gas Mark 6. Cut the dough into 5mm/¼in thick slices and arrange a batch on an ungreased baking sheet, leaving about 5cm/2in space around the crackers.

Bake for 5-7 minutes, or until golden brown. Carefully transfer the crackers with a fish slice to wire racks lined with kitchen paper to let them cool. Bake more batches in the same way. These are particularly good with celery sticks. (These crackers will keep in an airtight tin for up to 2 weeks, but are best when fresh.)

Miniature Scotch Eggs

Plain flour for coating
24 quails' eggs
350g/12oz minced pork
350g/12oz minced veal
1 tbsp finely chopped fresh
  parsley
2 tbsp chopped fresh chives
2 tsp dry mustard
½ tsp cayenne pepper
Salt and black pepper

2 eggs, beaten
Dry white breadcrumbs
Oil, for deep frying
Prepared English mustard,
  to serve

To Garnish
Lettuce leaves
Cucumber slices

illustrated on page 59

Makes 24

Place the quails' eggs in a pan of warm water to soak for 5-10 minutes to guard against cracking. Drain and replace in cold water. Bring to the boil, stirring a little to centre the yolks and to keep the eggs from cracking. Simmer for 4 minutes, then drain and plunge the eggs in cold water.

In a bowl, combine the meats, herbs, mustard, cayenne and seasoning to taste. Knead vigorously with the hands to mash the meat finely. Divide the mixture into 24 balls.

Drain the eggs and peel them. Roll the eggs in flour and shake off the excess. Take a ball of meat and form it around an egg, smoothing it into an oval. Repeat with the remaining meat and eggs. Dip the Scotch eggs into beaten egg and coat in the breadcrumbs.

Deep fry in hot oil, 8 at a time, until golden. Drain on kitchen paper and serve hot or at room temperature with a bowl of English mustard. Garnish the dish with lettuce and cucumber slices.

Cider-baked lamb cutlets.

Cider-Baked Lamb Cutlets

16 trimmed lamb cutlets
250ml/8fl oz dry cider
2 tbsp orange marmalade
Salt and black pepper
1 tbsp chopped fresh thyme

1 tbsp chopped fresh
*   rosemary leaves*

To Garnish
Fresh rosemary sprigs
Orange slices

illustrated on page 63

Makes 16

Preheat the oven to 200°C/400°F/Gas Mark 6. Place the cutlets in a baking dish in one layer, and pour over the cider. Spread each chop with a little of the marmalade and sprinkle with seasoning to taste, the thyme and rosemary.

Bake the chops for 25 minutes, or until browned on the outside and just pink inside, basting occasionally with the cider. Remove from the oven, dip in the cider one more time, shake off the excess, and arrange on a serving platter. Garnish with rosemary sprigs and orange slices, and serve.

Champagne Brunch

Menu

Mini-Sweetcorn 'Oysters' with Maple Syrup

Mushrooms on Toast

Melon Baskets

Poached Quail's Eggs in Cherry Tomatoes

Baby Bangers 'n' Mash

Hash-Stuffed Peaches

Devilled Ham in Eggs

Clockwise from the left: melon baskets, poached quails' eggs in cherry tomatoes, mushrooms on toast, hash-stuffed peaches, baby bangers 'n' mash, mini-sweetcorn 'oysters' with maple syrup.

Mini-Sweetcorn 'Oysters' with Maple Syrup

3 eggs
225g/8oz frozen sweetcorn, thawed and drained
4 tbsp plain flour
1 tsp caster sugar
60g/2oz butter, melted
Salt
4 tbsp sunflower oil
Maple syrup, to serve

illustrated on page 65

Makes about 20

In a large bowl, beat together the eggs, sweetcorn, flour, sugar and 15g/½oz of the melted butter. Add salt to taste.

Mix together the remaining butter and the oil. Pour 3½ tablespoons of this mixture into a hot 30cm/12in frying pan placed over medium heat. When the fat is bubbling, drop tablespoons of the sweetcorn mixture on to the pan to make 5cm/2in rounds. Add as many rounds as you can to the pan without overcrowding.

Cook the 'oysters' for about 3 minutes on one side, or until the bases are browned and the tops look drier. Turn with a fish slice and cook for a further 2 minutes or until done. Keep warm while cooking the other 'oysters', using the remaining fat.

Warm the syrup over low heat and pour into a bowl. Arrange the mini-'oysters' on a platter and serve with the bowl of syrup for dipping.

Mushrooms on Toast

450g/1 lb fresh button mushrooms (about 24)
150g/5oz butter
6 slices of white toast, cut into 2.5cm/1in squares
Juice of ½ lemon
2 tbsp finely chopped fresh parsley

illustrated on page 65

Makes about 24

Trim the mushrooms, wipe them with a damp cloth and pat dry. Melt 30g/1oz butter in a frying pan and sauté the toast squares until golden on both sides. Drain on kitchen paper.

Wipe out the frying pan to remove crumbs, then melt the remaining butter in it. Add the mushrooms and sauté in the butter until they are soft-ened slightly. Pour over the lemon juice and the finely chopped parsley, toss with the mushrooms, and remove from the heat.

Use a cocktail stick to skewer a mushroom on to a toast square. Repeat with the remaining mushrooms and squares. Serve immediately.

Melon Baskets

2 large Charentais melons
1 large honeydew or ogen melon
225g/8oz strawberries
12-14 fresh or canned lychees (or other small fruit)

illustrated on page 64

Makes 2

Plunge a sharp knife sideways into the centre of one Charentais melon. Slide the knife sideways through the melon until almost reaching the quarterway point on the perimeter, but stop 2.5cm/1in short. Slide the knife in the opposite direction, leaving the same border. Turn the melon round and follow the same procedure, stopping 2.5cm/1in from the quarter point (and thus leaving a base for a 2.5cm/1in handle), making sure that the knife has sliced through the fruit.

Then use the knife to cut a right angle to the previous cut, slicing down along the 'handle line', through the melon to reach the centre cut. Continue until you have outlined one side of the 'handle', and are able to remove a large wedge from one side of the melon. Do the same on the other side of the handle. Then carefully cut out the inside of the handle with the knife. Remove the seeds from the centre of the melon, then discard. Finally, using a melon baller, remove the flesh from the centre of the melon. Use the baller to shape the excess cut from the handle into balls. If liked, use a sharp knife to scallop or zigzag the edge of the basket. Reserve the basket and the balls. Repeat the process with the second Charentais melon.

Cut the honeydew or ogen melon in half. Remove the seeds and discard, Using the melon baller, shape the flesh into balls. Hull the strawberries and halve if large. If using fresh lychees, peel them and remove the stones, if liked.

Mix the orange and green melon balls with the strawberries and lychees and arrange attractively in the two melon baskets. (These can be made ahead and chilled, covered, for several hours.)

Poached Quails' Eggs in Cherry Tomatoes

12 large firm cherry tomatoes or small Canary tomatoes	Salt and black pepper
	1 packet (12) quails' eggs
3 fresh basil leaves	Fresh basil sprigs, to garnish

illustrated on page 65

Makes 12

Choose tomatoes that are just large enough to hold a quail's egg.

Preheat the oven to 180°C/350°F/Gas Mark 4. Cut off the stalk end of each tomato and scoop out the seeds carefully with a small spoon or melon scoop. Cut a small piece off the base of each tomato so that it will stand up. Cut each basil leaf into 4 pieces and put one into each tomato. Season with salt and pepper to taste, and carefully crack a quail's egg into it.

Place the tomatoes carefully on an oiled baking tray and bake for about 10 minutes or until the eggs are just set (don't let them get hard). Serve immediately, garnished with sprigs of basil.

Baby Bangers 'n' Mash

3x 225g/8 oz packets chipolata sausages (24), browned and cooked	2 tbsp double cream
	½ tsp cayenne pepper
2 large potatoes, peeled and cooked	1 tsp Dijon mustard
	1 egg, beaten
15g/½ oz butter	Fresh parsley sprigs, to garnish

illustrated on page 65

Makes 24

Preheat the oven to 200°C/400°F/Gas Mark 6. Split the cooked sausages carefully along their length.

Mash the potatoes with the butter, then add the cream, cayenne pepper, mustard and beaten egg. Combine thoroughly. Put into a piping bag fitted with a decorative tube and pipe the potato filling into the split sausages. (The sausages may be prepared up to this point and chilled for up to 3 days.)

Place the sausages on a baking tray and bake for about 20 minutes. Serve immediately garnished with parsley.

Hash-Stuffed Peaches

8 small ripe peaches or nectarines	½ tsp dried sage
	½ tsp dried basil
300g/10oz pork sausagemeat, cooked and drained	Salt and black pepper
	120ml/4fl oz double cream
	60g/2oz butter
2 small or 1 large sweet potato, cooked and finely chopped	3 tbsp peach or apricot jam
	Fresh sage leaves, to garnish
1 green pepper, seeded and finely chopped	

illustrated on page 65

Makes 16

Peel the peaches or nectarines; cut them in half and remove the stones. Set aside.

In a large bowl, combine the cooked sausagemeat, the sweet potato, onion, green pepper, sage, basil and seasoning to taste. Stir in the cream.

Melt half the butter in a frying pan and spoon the sausagemeat mixture into it. Press it down and brown until crusty on one side, about 5 minutes. Remove the sausagemeat hash, add the remaining butter, and brown the other side.

Spoon a little hash into each fruit half. Glaze with the jam melted over a low heat and garnish with a sage leaf. Serve warm.

Devilled Ham in Eggs

8 hard-boiled eggs	1½ tbsp chopped sour gherkin
120ml/4oz mayonnaise	
2tsp Dijon mustard	120g/4oz cooked ham, finely chopped
1tsp Worcestershire sauce	
Salt and black pepper	1 tbsp paprika

Makes 16

Shell the eggs carefully, cut them in half lengthways and scoop out the yolks into a bowl; reserve the egg whites.

Mash the yolks thoroughly with a fork. Stir in the mayonnaise, mustard, Worcestershire sauce, and salt and pepper to taste, mixing well. Fold in the sour gherkin and chopped ham. Mound the mixture into the egg whites. Dust the stuffed eggs with paprika and arrange on a serving platter.

French Hors d'Oeuvres

This celebratory collection reaches right across the map of France to include characteristic mini-dishes from Paris (Croque-Monsieurs), Provence (Fennel-Scented Olives, Tapenade and Crudités with Aïoli), the Basque Country (Spicy Stuffed Mushrooms), Alsace (Sauerkraut Balls) and Gascony (Prune Surprises). The tastes of the French are so catholic, that it is hard to find a herb or style of cooking which has eluded their culinary palette. What could be a better complement than red, white, or rosé wine – perhaps France's most cherished gift to the table?

Tarragon Cream Eggs

6 hard-boiled eggs, shelled
4 tbsp mayonnaise
1 tbsp fromage frais
1 tsp tarragon vinegar
Salt and black pepper
2 tsp finely chopped fresh
  tarragon leaves

To Garnish
½ red onion, finely chopped
Tarragon sprigs

illustrated on page 69

Makes 12

Halve the eggs lengthways and remove the yolks; reserve the whites. Mash the yolks thoroughly, then beat in the mayonnaise, *fromage frais*, vinegar, seasoning to taste, and chopped tarragon. Mix until thoroughly combined.

Spoon or pipe some of the filling into each of the eggwhite halves, and garnish with red onion and sprigs of tarragon.

Garlic Courgette Curls

3 courgettes
120g/4oz fresh parsley,
  chopped
2 garlic cloves
3 slices of bread, crusts
  removed and shredded

2½ tbsp grated Parmesan
  cheese
1 heaped tbsp mayonnaise
1 egg
Salt and pepper

illustrated on page 69

Makes about 15

Using the slicing blade of a food processor or a very sharp knife, cut the courgettes lengthways into slices, about 3mm/⅛in thick. Plunge the slices into boiling water for a few seconds just to soften, then remove and drain on kitchen paper. They will become more flexible as they stand.

Preheat the oven to 220°C/425°F/Gas Mark 7. In the bowl of a food processor, combine the parsley, garlic cloves, bread, 1½ tablespoons Parmesan, the mayonnaise and egg. Process until thoroughly mixed. Season to taste.

Lay out the courgette slices on a work surface. Place a teaspoonful of the parsley mixture on one end of each slice and roll up, securing with a wooden cocktail stick. Arrange the rolls on a baking sheet, sprinkle the tops with the remaining Parmesan and bake for 5-10 minutes or until the tops are browned and the curls cooked through. Serve warm.

Clockwise from the top: *fennel-scented olives, tarragon cream eggs, garlic courgette curls, finger Croque-Monsieurs, spicy stuffed mushrooms.*

Black and White Florentines

120g/4oz butter
90g/3oz caster sugar
2 tbsp double cream,
  whipped
60g/2oz chopped candied
  peel

60g/2oz glacé cherries,
  chopped
60g/2oz flaked almonds
60g/2oz shelled walnuts,
  chopped
90g/3oz plain chocolate
90g/3oz white chocolate

illustrated on page 73

Makes about 25

Preheat the oven to 180°C/350°F/Gas Mark 4. Line baking sheets with baking parchment.

In a saucepan over low heat, melt the butter. Stir in the sugar, and when that has dissolved, stir in the whipped cream. Bring to the boil and cook, stirring, for 1 minute. Take the saucepan off the heat and stir in the candied peel, cherries, almonds and walnuts until well mixed.

Drop teaspoonfuls of the mixture on to the paper-lined baking sheets, about 4-5 well apart as they will spread. Bake for 10 minutes or until rich brown and bubbling. Take the sheets from the oven, and allow to cool slightly, then carefully remove the florentines to wire racks with a fish slice. Leave until completely cold.

In a bowl over hot water, gently melt the plain chocolate. Spread some of the chocolate over the bases of half of the florentines, and use a fork to make wavy lines across the chocolate. Repeat the process with the white chocolate. If liked, leave some biscuits plain. Let the chocolate harden, then serve, or store in an airtight tin for up to 2 weeks.

Tapenade Toasts

120g/40z Italian or Greek
  black olives, stones
60g/2oz green olives,
  stoned
1 garlic clove
2 tbsp capers, drained
3 tbsp tuna in oil, drained
4 anchovy fillets

1 tsp fresh lemon juice
Large handful of fresh basil
  leaves
125ml/4fl oz extra virgin
  olive oil
2 thin French baguettes
12 cherry tomatoes, each
  cut into 4 rounds

Makes about 24

In the bowl of a food processor with a metal blade, combine all the ingredients except the oil, bread and cherry tomatoes. Process until smooth. With the motor running, slowly pour in the oil, until you have a thick, rich consistency. (The tapenade may be made ahead and chilled for 2-3 days.)

Preheat the oven to 180°C/350°F/Gas Mark 4. Slice the baguettes into 12 slices each and spread out on a baking sheet. Toast the slices in the oven for about 15 minutes, turning once. (These can be made ahead and kept in an airtight container for up to 2 weeks.)

Preheat the grill. Spread the tapenade on the toast slices. Position two slices of overlapping tomato in the corner of each slice, and grill for about 4 minutes, until the tapenade is hot and the tomatoes softened and bubbling. Arrange on a platter and serve.

Alsatian Cocktail Balls

1 large potato (about
  225g/8oz)
Small knob of unsalted
  butter
4 tbsp milk
Salt and black pepper
350g/12oz sauerkraut,
  rinsed, squeezed dry and
  shaken out
1 tsp Dijon mustard

120g/4oz salt beef, chopped
3 tbsp finely chopped fresh
  chives
1 small red onion, finely
  chopped
1 egg
120g/4oz fresh
  breadcrumbs
Sunflower oil, for deep
  frying

Makes about 25

Peel the potato, cut it into chunks and cook in boiling salted water until tender. Drain, then mash the potato with the butter, milk and seasoning to taste, until smooth. Stir the sauerkraut, mustard, salt beef, chives and red onion into the mashed potato.

Take a walnut sized portion of the mixture and shape it into a ball. Continue until all the dough has been used. Chill the balls, covered, for at least 2 hours. (The balls may be made ahead up to this point and kept, chilled, for 2 days.)

Beat the egg with a little water. Dip the balls into the egg wash, then roll in the breadcrumbs to coat all over. Deep-fry in the hot oil in batches of 5 until golden brown. Drain on kitchen paper and serve warm.

Crudités with Aïoli

Crudités with aïoli.

2 red peppers, seeded and
cut into chunks
24 baby new potatoes,
boiled
1 small cauliflower, cut into
florets
24 small carrots, trimmed
12 celery stalks, trimmed
and cut in half
24 cherry tomatoes
24 spring onions, trimmed

Aïoli
10 garlic cloves, crushed
Salt and white pepper
2 egg yolks, at room
temperature
250ml/8fl oz extra virgin
olive oil
1 tbsp Dijon mustard
2 tbsp fresh lemon juice

illustrated on page 71

Serves 12

Make the *aïoli:* with an electric mixer on high speed, beat the crushed garlic, salt and pepper to taste and the egg yolks until well combined. Beat in a few drops of oil, then add the mustard and lemon juice. Continue adding the oil in a thin stream, beating constantly. Transfer some of the *aïoli* to a serving bowl and keep the rest in reserve for replenishing. Chill for at least 2 hours or up to 24 to let the flavours combine.

Meanwhile, prepare all the vegetables. Arrange them attractively and serve with the *aïoli*.

Spicy Stuffed Mushrooms

24 medium brown-cap mushrooms	60g/2oz stoned black olives, chopped
225g/8oz sausagemeat	60g/2oz fresh parsley, finely chopped
¼ tsp dried sage	
Pinch of cayenne pepper	3 tbsp mayonnaise
¼ tsp fennel seeds	1-2 tbsp crema di peperoni or chilli sauce
1 small onion, finely chopped	Black olives, quartered, to garnish
1 garlic clove, crushed	
1 tbsp olive oil	

illustrated on page 69

Makes 24

Wipe the mushrooms with a damp cloth and pat dry. Remove the stalks.

Crumble the sausagemeat into a frying pan and brown over medium heat, stirring in the sage, cayenne pepper and fennel seeds. When the meat is cooked through, drain off the fat and turn the meat into a bowl. Return the pan to the heat, add the onion, garlic and oil and sauté until the onion is softened and lightly coloured. Scrape the pan contents into the sausagemeat and add the chopped olives and parsley. Combine thoroughly, then stir in the mayonnaise and *crema di peperoni*. (The filling may be prepared up to this point and kept, chilled and covered, for up to 2 days.)

Preheat the oven to 220°C/425°F/Gas Mark 7. Arrange the mushroom caps on a lightly oiled baking sheet and pile a little of the filling into each of them. Bake for 15 minutes, or until bubbling and browned. Garnish the tops with quartered black olives, and arrange on a flat dish. Leave for 5-10 minutes before serving.

Finger Croque-Monsieurs

300g/10oz Gruyère cheese, finely grated	16 slices of white bread, crusts removed
4 tbsp soured cream	8 slices of cooked ham
1½ tbsp Dijon mustard	120g/4oz butter, melted
½ tsp brandy	

illustrated on page 69

Makes 24

In a large bowl, thoroughly combine 225g/8oz of the Gruyère, the soured cream, mustard and brandy. Lay out the bread slices and spread generously with the mixture. On top of 8 slices place the ham slices, and then the remaining bread slices, spread-side down. (This can be prepared 2-3 days ahead of time.)

Brush the tops of the sandwiches with half the butter and cut into thirds. Fry, brushed side down, over medium heat until golden. Brush the tops with more butter, turn and cook until the cheese has just melted. Keep warm in a low oven while frying the remaining sandwiches in the same way.

Preheat the grill to high.

Sprinkle the tops of all the fingers with the remaining Gruyère and grill for 2-3 minutes until the tops are bubbling. Arrange the fingers on a platter and serve warm.

Prune Surprises

175ml/6fl oz Cognac	12 sheets of phyllo pastry, each about 20x30cm/8x12in
12 ready-to-eat stoned prunes	
75g/2½ oz butter, melted	1 tbsp Demarara sugar
5 tbsp sunflower oil	Icing sugar, to finish

illustrated on page 73

Makes 12

In a saucepan, combine the Cognac and prunes. Bring to the boil, then remove from the heat and leave to steep, covered and chilled, for 24 hours.

Drain the prunes as thoroughly as possible. Preheat the oven to 190°C/375°F/Gas Mark 5. In a bowl, combine the melted butter with the oil.

Take one sheet of the phyllo (keep the rest covered with a damp cloth to prevent them from drying out), brush it with the oil mixture and fold the long end over to make an approximate square. Place a prune in the centre, sprinkling with a little sugar and bring up the ends of the phyllo over the top. Twist to form a pouch. Pull back the edge of the bunched phyllo attractively and trim, if needed. Brush with the oil mixture and set on a baking sheet. Repeat with the remaining prunes and phyllo.

Bake the prune pouches for 10-15 minutes, or until the phyllo is golden. Remove from the sheet and allow to cool, then dredge with sifted icing sugar. Serve immediately or keep, covered tightly, for several hours.

Left: *prune surprises*. Right: *black and white Florentines.*

Fennel-Scented Olives

450g/1 lb green olives in
 brine
1½ tsp fennel seeds

Pared zest from 1 large
 orange, cut into strips
4-5cm/1½-2in long
1½ tbsp sherry vinegar

---

illustrated on page 69

Serves about 16

Drain the olives, reserving the brine. Place the olives in a bowl, together with the fennel seeds, orange zest and vinegar. Mix together well. Pour over the reserved brine, and add a little water, if necessary, to cover. Cover tightly and chill for at least 24 hours or up to 2 weeks. Stir occasionally to distribute the flavours.

Drain the olives before serving with the fennel seeds and orange zest.

Chinese Dim Sum

Dim Sum literally means 'Dot on the Heart' – an indication of their ability to please and satisfy. They are usually served in Chinese restaurants from lunch through tea-time and, though accompanied by chopsticks, many are bite-sized and ideal as finger food. The dim sum in our selection have been somewhat adapted to omit the laborious preparation and deft execution required by some Chinese specialities. Exotic punches and mixed drinks are capable foils for the range of spices and textures found here.

Sweet Fried Nuts

120g/4oz Demerara sugar
120g/4oz shelled unsalted cashews

120g/4oz shelled unsalted macadamia nuts
Sunflower oil

illustrated on page 75

Makes 225g/8oz

In a large saucepan, combine the sugar and the nuts. Pour over 250ml/8fl oz cold water. Bring to the boil over high heat, stirring to dissolve the sugar, then lower the heat slightly and simmer until the water has evaporated and the nuts are coated and shiny but not caramelized. Stir, especially towards the end, to protect against burning. Drain the nuts.

Heat oil in a large frying pan until very hot. Add the nuts and fry, stirring, until they are golden brown. Drain on kitchen paper. Allow to cool, then serve warm or at room temperature. (They will keep for about 2 weeks in an airtight tin.)

Spicy Meat in Chinese Leaves

2 tbsp long-grain rice
225g/8oz minced pork
4 tbsp fresh lemon juice
6 tbsp beef consommé
4 tbsp Oriental fish sauce (nuoc mam or nam pla)
2 tsp chilli powder
4 spring onions, chopped

1 stalk of lemon grass, finely sliced
Juice of 1 lime
1 tbsp anise seeds
20 Chinese leaves
Fresh coriander sprigs, to garnish

illustrated on page 77

Makes 20

In a frying pan over low heat, fry the rice *without* oil, stirring, until pale brown. In the bowl of a food processor fitted with a metal blade, process the rice until finely ground; set aside. In the food processor, blend the pork until it is a paste.

In the frying pan, combine the lemon juice, consommé, fish sauce and chilli powder and bring to the boil. Stir in the pork paste and cook until the paste is brown and broken up and the liquid has almost evaporated. Stir in the spring onions, lemon grass, ground rice, lime juice and anise seeds and cook for a few seconds more. Remove from the heat. (This dish may be prepared to this point and kept, chilled for up to 2 days.)

Allow the meat mixture to cool to room temperature, then spoon it into the Chinese leaves. Garnish with coriander. Carefully arrange on a platter so that the contents do not spill from the leaves.

Clockwise from the top: rice croquettes with hot dripping sauce, sweet fried nuts, char chiu buns, prawn toasts.

74

Char Chiu Buns

1 tbsp tahini paste	**Dough**
3 tbsp soy sauce	1½ tsp dried yeast or one
2 tbsp chilli sauce	sachet of easy blend dried
3 tbsp golden syrup	yeast
2 spring onions, finely	225g/8oz plain flour
chopped	Sesame oil
2 tsp sesame oil	
2 tbsp dry sherry	**To Serve**
4 slices of fresh root ginger,	Shredded spring onions
skinned and shredded	Prepared hoisin or plum
1 tsp five spice powder	sauce
Salt and pepper	
2 small pork fillets, trimmed	

illustrated on page 75

Makes 12

In a saucepan, heat the tahini paste with the soy and chilli sauces and the golden syrup. When warm and thoroughly blended, take off the heat and stir in the spring onions, sesame oil, sherry, ginger, five spice powder and seasoning to taste. Pour into a large bowl add 300ml/½ pint water and stir to combine thoroughly.

Score the pork fillets four times each and immerse in the marinade. Leave in a cool place for at least 6 hours or overnight.

To make the dough, dissolve the yeast in 150ml/ ¼ pint of lukewarm water. Stir in 60g/2oz of the flour and leave in a warm place for about 30 minutes or until foamy. If using easy-blend yeast, follow the directions on the packet.

Stir in the remaining flour. Knead with the hands until the dough is elastic. Break into 12 equal pieces and shape into buns. Brush with sesame oil. Leave to rise for 15-30 minutes until slightly puffy.

Steam in bamboo steamers or in a large saucepan with a steaming rack for 10 minutes, until glossy. The buns will be pale. Cool on wire racks.

Preheat the oven to 230°C/450°F/Gas Mark 8. Remove the pork from the marinade and squeeze off excess with the hands. Pass a large skewer lengthways through each fillet and suspend from an oven rack placed at the top of the oven, with a baking tin underneath to catch drips. Roast for about 35 minutes, until cooked but not too dry.

Remove the skewers. Let the pork rest for 10 minutes, then cut across into thin slices. While still warm, divide the pork slices among the split buns. Serve with a little shredded spring onion and sauce (either hoisin or plum).

Rice Croquettes with Hot Dipping Sauce

120g/4oz onion, chopped	Groundnut oil, for deep
15g/½ oz butter	frying
2 tsp sesame oil	Fresh coriander sprigs, to
225g/8oz long-grain rice	garnish
2 tbsp finely chopped fresh	
coriander	**Dipping Sauce**
600ml/1 pint chicken stock	175ml/6fl oz rice vinegar
1 egg	4 tbsp soy sauce
30g/1oz desiccated coconut	1 tsp chopped fresh chives
25g/¾ oz cream cheese	½ tsp caster sugar
1 tsp ground cumin	Large dash of hot chilli
Salt and black pepper	sauce
60-90g/2-3oz dry	½ tsp sesame oil
breadcrumbs	

illustrated on page 75

Makes 14

Make the dipping sauce first: in a bowl combine all the ingredients and keep chilled.

In a frying pan, sauté the onion in the butter until softened. Add the sesame oil and the rice and stir until glazed. Stir in the coriander and stock. Bring to the boil, then cover, reduce the heat and simmer for about 20 minutes, or until the rice has absorbed all the liquid and is tender.

Take off the heat and stir in the egg, coconut, cream cheese, cumin and salt and pepper to taste. The mixture should be moist. Shape into croquettes, roll in the breadcrumbs and chill for at least one hour. (The croquettes may be made to this point up to 2 days ahead).

Heat a deep pan of groundnut oil until very hot. Drop in the croquettes, 4-5 at a time and fry until golden and crisp all over. Remove with a slotted spoon and drain on kitchen paper. Serve warm, garnished with coriander, with the dipping sauce.

Hot Sweet and Sour Chicken Drumsticks

5 tbsp hot chilli sauce	*1 tbsp brown sugar*
4 tbsp dry sherry	*60g/2oz raisins*
2 tbsp fresh lemon juice	*6 garlic cloves, chopped*
4 tbsp tomato ketchup	*18 chicken drumsticks*

Makes 18

Spicy meat in Chinese leaves.

In the bowl of a blender or food processor, combine all ingredients except the chicken and process until you have a wet paste. Place the drumsticks in a shallow baking dish and cover with the paste, turning to coat. Cover and refrigerate for at least 3 hours or overnight.

Preheat the oven to 200°C/400°F/Gas Mark 6. Place the coated chicken on a well-greased baking sheet. Bake for about 20 minutes, until the chicken is browned and cooked through. Serve warm.

Prawn Toasts

450g/1lb peeled prawns,
  raw or cooked
3 garlic cloves, chopped
4 spring onions, chopped
1cm/½ in piece fresh root
  ginger, chopped
Salt and pepper
1 tbsp cornflour

3 tbsp dry sherry
1 tbsp sesame oil
30g/1oz lard
2 egg whites
10 slices of white bread,
  crusts removed
60g/2oz sesame seeds
Groundnut oil, for frying

illustrated on page 75

Makes 40

Raw prawns are preferable in this recipe, but if they are unavailable, use cooked ones. Rinse the prawns and dry thoroughly before using.

In a food processor with a metal blade, combine the garlic, spring onions, ginger, cornflour, sherry, sesame oil and salt and pepper to taste. Process to combine. Add the prawns and lard and process until smooth. Add the egg whites and process until all the ingredients are combined.

On a work surface, lay out the bread slices and divide the prawn mixture among them. Spread evenly over the slices, then dip the coated side in the sesame seeds. Chill the slices, covered, for 1 hour or until ready to cook. (If not used on the same day, the slices can be frozen and then fried without thawing.)

Heat groundnut oil in a frying pan and fry the slices one by one, until both sides are golden. Drain on kitchen paper and keep warm while frying the remaining slices. Cut each toast into quarters and serve immediately.

Cantonese Almond Biscuits

45g/1½ oz white vegetable
  fat
90g/3oz castor sugar
1 size-4 egg
45g/1½ oz plain flour
Salt

30g/1oz sweetened
  desiccated coconut
Dash of almond essence
Pinch of five spice powder
20 unskinned almonds,
  halved

illustrated on page 79

Makes about 35-40

In a bowl, cream the vegetable fat with an electric mixer. Slowly add the sugar, beating until the mixture is fluffy. Beat in the egg, then the flour and a pinch of salt. Combine thoroughly. With a spoon, stir in the coconut, almond essence and five spice powder. (This may be made ahead and kept, chilled and covered, for up to 3 days.)

Preheat the oven to 190°C/375°F/Gas Mark 5. Spoon teaspoonfuls of the mixture onto greased baking sheets, spacing them 2.5cm/1in apart. Make a slight indentation in each ball with your finger and press an almond half gently into it. Bake for about 6-7 minutes, until just the edges are golden. Leave to cool for 1-2 minutes on the sheets, then remove with a fish slice to wire racks to cool.

Serve at room temperature with the fresh fruit and the Cinnamon Dipping Sauce. (The biscuits may be made up to 2 weeks ahead and kept in an airtight tin.)

Fruit with Cinnamon Dipping Sauce

Left: fruit with cinnamon dipping sauce.
Right: Cantonese almond biscuits.

350ml/12fl oz plain Greek-style yogurt
3 tbsp light brown sugar
¾ tsp ground cinnamon
½ tsp ground ginger
Pinch of grated nutmeg
Little fresh lemon juice

Sliced strawberries, to decorate
Fresh fruit on sticks for dipping: strawberries, lychees, pineapple pieces, kumquats, etc.

---

illustrated on page 79

Makes about 350ml/12fl oz sauce

In a bowl, beat together the yogurt and brown sugar until the sugar is dissolved. Stir in the cinnamon, ginger, nutmeg and lemon juice. Whisk until thoroughly combined.

Serve the sauce in a bowl, decorated with strawberry slices and surrounded by the colourful fresh fruit threaded on cocktail sticks.

A Formal Cocktail Party

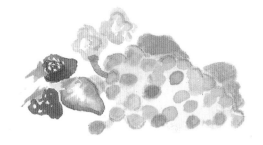

Menu

Nutty Apricot Mounds

Spiced Pistachio Brittle

Choux Buns with Smoked Trout Mouse

Dates with Cheese Stuffing

Crab and Prawn Palmiers

Devils on Horseback

Kabanos and Papaya Sticks

Clockwise from the left: *nutty apricot mounds, kabanos and papaya sticks, spiced pistachio brittle, devils on horseback, choux buns with smoked trout mousse, crab and prawn palmiers.*

Nutty Apricot Mounds

60g/2oz sesame seeds	2 tbsp dried onion flakes
30g/1oz smoked almonds	½ tsp curry powder
225g/8oz cream cheese	Salt and black pepper
2 tbsp grated Parmesan	25 ready-to-eat dried
cheese	apricots (about 150g/5oz)

illustrated on page 80

Makes about 25

Toast the sesame seeds in a frying pan over low to moderate heat until they are golden, about 5 minutes. Remove and cool. Meanwhile, finely chop or sliver the smoked almonds. Reserve.

In a bowl, combine the cheeses, onion flakes, curry powder and salt and pepper to taste. Beat until mixed. Add the sesame seeds and mix together well. (The filling can be made ahead and chilled for up to 2 days.)

Take an apricot and spoon a little of the cheese mixture on it, smoothing it into a mound. Press some of the chopped or slivered almonds over it. Repeat with the remaining apricots, cheese and nuts until all are used.

Arrange the mounds attractively on a plate and serve within a couple of hours.

Spiced Pistachio Brittle

225g/8oz shelled salted	1 tsp ground cinnamon
pistachios	1 tsp grated nutmeg
120g/4oz sugar	½ tsp cayenne pepper

illustrated on page 81

Makes about 225g/8oz

In a large frying pan over medium heat, stir and shake the pistachios until hot and golden, about 5-6 minutes. Sprinkle the sugar and spices over the nuts and cook for another 5 minutes, or until the sugar caramelizes and coats the nuts, stirring as necessary. Take great care not to let the caramelized sugar burn.

Pour the brittle on to an oiled baking tray and let it cool. Then break into small pieces and serve. This can be made well in advance and stored in an airtight container for up to 2 weeks.

Choux Buns with Smoked Trout Mousse

	Filling
75g/2½oz plain flour	1 smoked trout, skinned
Salt	and boned
4 tbsp milk	30g/1oz butter, softened
60g/2oz butter	120g/4oz cream cheese
2 eggs, beaten	2 tbsp fresh lemon juice
Mustard and cress, to	1 tbsp prepared horseradish
garnish	Salt and black pepper

illustrated on page 81

Makes about 25

Preheat the oven to 220°C/425°F/Gas Mark 7.

To make the choux buns, sift together the flour and salt to taste. Make up the milk to 150ml/¼pint with water. In a saucepan, combine the butter and milk and water mixture. Heat gently until the butter melts, then raise the heat and bring to the boil. Take the pan off the heat and pour in the salted flour. Stir quickly with a wooden spoon until the flour has been absorbed, then beat until the dough is smooth and draws away from the sides of the pan. Do not overbeat.

Allow the mixture to cool slightly, then gradually beat in the eggs. The dough should be thick and shiny. Spoon it into a piping bag fitted with a 1cm/⅛in plain vegetable tube. Pipe about 25 bun shapes on greased baking sheets. Bake for about 12-15 minutes, or until the choux buns are puffed and crisp. Remove to a wire rack to cool.

While the buns are cooling, make the filling. (Alternatively, make the filling ahead and chill, covered, for up to 1 day.) Put the trout, butter, cream cheese, lemon juice and horseradish into the bowl of a blender or food processor fitted with a metal blade. Process until smooth, then season to taste.

Split the choux buns open, not cutting all the way through. Spoon the mousse filling into a piping bag fitted with a star tube or simply use a teaspoon. Fill each of the split buns with a little of the smoked trout mousse. Arrange attractively on a plate and serve, garnished with mustard and cress.

Dates with Cheese Stuffing

120g/4oz Roquefort or	1 tbsp brandy
Danish blue cheese	30 plump dates, stoned
60g/2oz cream cheese	Paprika
30g/1oz butter, softened	

Makes 16-18

Mash together the blue cheese, cream cheese, butter and brandy, working until thoroughly combined. Gently force open the hole left by the stone in each date and stuff with the cheese filling. Sprinkle a little paprika on top of the cheese. These may be kept chilled for up to 1 day.

Crab and Prawn Palmiers

225g/8oz puff pastry,
  thawed if frozen
1 egg, beaten with a little
  milk
Fresh dill sprigs, to garnish

Filling
1 tbsp sunflower oil
10g/⅓oz butter
2 garlic cloves, crushed

3 spring onions, finely
  chopped
120g/4oz cooked peeled
  prawns, finely chopped
120g/4oz cooked white
  crabmeat, finely chopped
1 tbsp plain flour
Salt and black pepper
1 tbsp chopped fresh dill

illustrated on page 80

Makes 25-30

To make the filling, heat the oil and butter together in a frying pan, add the garlic and spring onions and sauté over a low heat until soft and just coloured. Stir in the prawns and crab meat and heat through. Add the flour and stir in for 1 minute, then add 2 tablespoons water and cook until thickened. Remove from the heat and stir in salt and pepper to taste and the chopped dill.

Roll out the puff pastry to a 35 x 25cm/14 x 10in rectangle. Cut it in half lengthways. Spread half the filling lengthways down the middle of each pastry strip. Fold over the long sides of each strip so that they meet in the middle over the filling. Brush the egg mixture over the pastry down the middle, then fold over each strip in half lengthways. Press down gently on each log. Cover and chill for at least 1 hour, or overnight.

Preheat the oven to 190°C/375°F/Gas mark 5. Brush the logs all over with the egg mixture, cut each log across into about 15 slices, and place the palmiers on oiled baking sheets. Bake for 12-15 minutes, or until golden brown. Remove from the baking sheets and allow to cool slightly before serving warm, garnished with sprigs of dill.

Devils on Horseback

225g/8oz plump, stoned
  ready-to-eat prunes
Mustard piccalilli
1 tbsp light brown sugar

225g/8oz streaky bacon,
  rind removed, cut into
  strips
Watercress sprigs, to
  garnish

illustrated on page 81

Makes about 25

Take a prune and open the stoned section. With a teaspoon, drop in a little piccalilli – either an onion or cauliflower piece or gherkin slice with some of the mustard sauce – and a pinch of brown sugar. Close the prune opening and wrap the prune in a bacon strip. Secure with a wooden cocktail stick. Repeat with the rest of the prunes, piccalilli and bacon. (These can be made ahead of time and chilled, covered, for up to 2 days.)

Preheat the grill to high.

Grill the devils for 5-8 minutes, turning once, until the bacon is cooked and crisp but not dry. Serve immediately, garnished with the watercress.

Kabanos and Papaya Sticks

4 kabanos sausages
2 large, firm papayas,
  peeled and seeded

Juice of 2 limes
Lime slices, to garnish

illustrated on page 81

Makes 24

Choose the kabanos sausages which are plump and fresh, not dry, wizened ones. They will produce a juicier effect.

Cut the sausages into 1cm/½in thick slices. Cut the papaya into 2.5cm/1in chunks. On small wooden skewers, thread one sausage slice, a papaya cube and another sausage slice. Repeat with the remaining kabanos and papaya. (The sticks may be made ahead and chilled overnight.)

Preheat the grill to high.

Cook the sticks for about 5 minutes, turning once, until the meat and fruit are hot and glazed. Dip each stick into the lime juice and serve immediately, garnished with lime slices.

Indian Tiffin

It is a much-publicised truism that the curries, biriyanis and other spicy dishes that we so enjoy in this country do not exist on the subcontinent. Real native Indian cooking for snacks and appetisers makes much use of deep-frying and the tandoori oven; the latter achieves a result halfway between grilling and baking. Despite the lack of such authentic equipment, our Indian offerings here celebrate the marriage of East and West with a few Anglo-Indian influenced dishes, as well as those likely to be found in better-off homes in Western and Southern India.

Split and Chick Pea Nibbles

150g/5oz dried yellow split peas	*¾ tsp chilli powder*
90/3oz dried chick peas	*½ tsp ground cumin*
2½ tsp bicarbonate of soda	*½ tsp ground coriander*
Groundnut oil, for deep frying	*1 tsp garlic salt*
	Pinch of ground cinnamon
	Pinch of ground cloves

Makes about 225g/8oz

Rinse the split and chick peas, pick over and drain. Cover with cold water, add the bicarbonate of soda and leave to soak overnight.

Drain the peas, rinse again and drain thoroughly. Turn on to kitchen paper to dry for 1 hour.

Heat enough oil to make a 6cm/2½ in deep layer in a deep fryer. When very hot, deep fry the peas, in batches, until golden but not too dry – about 90 seconds. Lift out each batch with a slotted spoon and drain on kitchen paper.

When the peas are drained, move them to a shallow dish. Mix together all spices and sprinkle over the peas, tossing to combine. Cool the peas, and serve in small bowls. (The peas will keep in an air-tight jar for up to 2 weeks.)

Goanese Stuffed Courgettes

8 small courgettes, halved lengthways	*2 small tomatoes, skinned, seeded and finely chopped*
2 tbsp olive oil	*175g/6oz cooked basmati rice*
1 onion, finely chopped	*Salt and black pepper*
2 garlic cloves, finely chopped	
1 tsp mustard seeds	**To garnish**
½ tsp ground turmeric	*Tomato slices*
2 tbsp fresh lemon juice	*Fresh parsley*
5 cardamom pods, cracked	

illustrated on page 85

Makes 16

Steam the halved courgettes over boiling water for 3-5 minutes, or until they are just tender. Scoop out the centres, chop the flesh and reserve both the shells and the chopped flesh.

Heat the oil in a small frying pan and sauté the onion and garlic until softened and lightly coloured. Add the mustard seeds, turmeric, lemon juice and cardamom; stir over the heat for 1 minute. Add the chopped courgette flesh and the chopped tomatoes and stir until most of the liquid has evaporated. Stir in the rice and season to taste with salt and pepper. (If liked, discard the cardamom pods.) Divide the filling among the 16 courgette halves, patting it in.

Preheat the oven to 180°C/350°F/Gas Mark 4. Place the courgettes on lightly oiled baking trays and bake for 20-25 minutes. Remove and allow to cool. Serve just warm or at room temperature, garnished with sliced tomato and parsley. (The stuffed courgettes can be made ahead, covered and chilled for up to 2 days.)

Clockwise from the top: *spiced chicken samosas, Goanese stuffed courgettes, almond lamb kebabs, creamy eggs in bread cases.*

Spiced Chicken Samosas

200g/7oz plain flour
1 egg white, lightly beaten
Groundnut oil, for deep frying
Spring onions, cut into brushes, to garnish

Filling
1 garlic clove, crushed
1 small onion, finely chopped
1½ tsp grated fresh root ginger
1 tbsp sunflower oil
1 tbsp curry powder
1 tbsp white wine vinegar
225g/8oz boneless, skinless chicken, finely chopped
2 tbsp finely chopped fresh coriander
Salt and black pepper
1 egg, beaten

illustrated on page 85

Makes about 30

In a saucepan, sauté the garlic, onion and ginger in the oil over medium heat for about 1 minute. Stir in the curry powder and sauté for another minute. Pour over the vinegar and stir to combine, then add the chicken. Simmer for 5 minutes, until the chicken is cooked through. Take the pan off the heat, and stir in the coriander, seasoning to taste, and the beaten egg. Set aside to cool.

Meanwhile make the pastry. Sift the flour into a bowl. Stir in 250ml/8fl oz boiling water. Work into a firm dough, then turn on to a floured work surface and knead gently until the dough in smooth and malleable. Cover and leave to rest for 20 minutes.

Pinch off half the dough and roll out thinly on a floured surface to make a large rectangle about 1-2cm/½–¾in thick. Cut out 8.5cm/3⅓in rounds from the dough; reroll the trimmings and cut out more rounds. Repeat with the second portion of dough.

Divide the chicken mixture in half. Place half of the dough rounds on the work surface and divide one portion of filling among them. Brush the edges of the rounds with egg white, fold in half and press to seal. Repeat with the remaining dough rounds and filling. (The pastries can be made ahead and kept, chilled, for up to 2 days.)

Heat oil until very hot and deep-fry the pastries, in batches of 5-6, until golden brown. Drain on kitchen paper and serve hot, garnished with spring onion brushes.

Curried Broccoli Fritters with Coriander Dip

120g/4oz plain flour
½ tsp curry powder
½ tsp ground coriander
¼ tsp ground cumin
Salt and black pepper
¼ tsp bicarbonate of soda
Large pinch of cayenne pepper
1 tbsp garlic paste
2 tbsp fresh lemon juice
175g/6oz trimmed broccoli, very finely chopped
120g/4oz onions, finely chopped
Groundnut oil, for deep frying
Lime slices, to garnish

Dipping Sauce
2 tbsp chopped fresh coriander
½ tsp cayenne pepper
1 tsp fresh lime juice
120ml/4fl oz plain Greek-style yoghurt

illustrated on page 87

Makes about 20 – 25

To make the sauce, combine the chopped coriander, cayenne, lime juice and yoghurt and whisk until mixed. Pour into a serving bowl. Sprinkle the top with cayenne, cover and chill until needed.

In a large bowl, mix together the flour, curry powder, coriander, cumin, salt and pepper to taste, the bicarbonate of soda and cayenne. Stir in 150ml/¼ pint water a little at a time, then the garlic paste and lemon juice. When well mixed, fold in the broccoli and onions. (The batter may be made ahead and kept, covered and chilled, for a few hours.)

Heat a deep pan of oil until very hot. Drop tablespoons of the batter into the oil and deep-fry, in batches of 5-6 at a time, for about 4 minutes. Drain on kitchen paper.

Arrange the fritters around the bowl of dipping sauce and serve immediately, garnished with lime slices.

Curried broccoli fritters with coriander dip.

Almond Lamb Kebabs

2 tbsp desiccated coconut
1 tbsp chopped almonds
1 onion, finely chopped
2 garlic cloves, finely
   chopped
1 tsp finely chopped fresh
   root ginger
¼ tsp ground cinnamon
¼ tsp ground cloves
¼ tsp ground cardamom

¼ tsp grated nutmeg
Salt and black pepper
6 tbsp plain yoghurt
450g/1lb boned lamb leg
   steaks, cut into small
   cubes

To garnish
Fresh coriander
Onion rings

---

illustrated on page 85

Makes 16

Preheat the oven to 220°C/425°F/Gas mark 7. Spread the coconut and almonds on a baking tray and toast in the oven until golden, watching carefully, about 5 minutes. Allow to cool.

Put the onion, garlic and ginger into the bowl of a food processor or blender and process to a smooth paste. Add the spices, salt and pepper to taste, the toasted coconut and almonds, and the yoghurt. Process again until combined and smooth.

Place the lamb cubes in a bowl and spoon over the spicy paste, rubbing it into the meat. Cover and chill overnight.

Preheat the grill to hot. Thread the meat on to small wooden skewers and grill, until cooked, about 4 minutes on each side. Serve warm, garnished with fresh coriander and onion rings.

Creamy Eggs in Bread Cases

12 slices of white bread
30g/1oz butter, melted
1½ tsp vegetable oil

Filling
45g/1½ oz unsalted butted
1 small onion, chopped
½ tsp grated fresh root
  ginger
1 fresh green chilli, finely
  chopped

½ tsp cumin seeds
1 tbsp finely chopped fresh
  coriander
1 small tomato, skinned,
  seeded and chopped
6 size-2 eggs, beaten

To garnish
6 stuffed green olives,
  sliced
Fresh chervil sprigs

illustrated on page 85

Makes 24

Preheat the oven to 180°C/350°F/Gas mark 4.

To make the bread cases, cut two 5cm/2in rounds from each slice. With a rolling pin, flatten the rounds, rolling back and forth, until the bread is very thin. Place 12 of the rounds in a greased 12-hole small bun tin. Brush with the mixed melted butter and oil, and place another tin on top to press the bread rounds into shape. Bake for 8-10 minutes, or until the bread cases are golden. Remove and cool. Repeat the process with the remaining bread rounds. (These can be made up to 2 days ahead and kept in an airtight container.)

For the filling, melt the butter in a saucepan over medium heat and sauté the onion until soft, then stir in the ginger, chilli, cumin seeds, fresh coriander and tomato. Cook until the tomato is soft. Stir in the eggs and season to taste. Turn the eggs over gently until they form soft, rich curds.

Take the eggs off the heat and fill each of the prepared bread cases. Serve still warm or at room temperature, garnished with an olive slice and a feathering of chervil.

Fruit-Topped Lemon Curd Tartlets

120g/4oz unsalted butter
120g/4oz caster sugar
2 tbsp grated fresh lemon
  zest
4 tbsp fresh lemon juice
2 size-2 eggs, beaten
1 kiwi fruit, sliced and cut
  into quarters

3 kumquats, thinly sliced

Pastry
175g/6oz plain flour
Salt
90g/3oz unsalted butter
30g/1oz white vegetable fat

illustrated on page 89

Makes 16

Cut the butter into small pieces and place in a double saucepan over hot water. Add the sugar, lemon zest and juice and eggs, and stir until the mixture is thick enough to coat the back of a wooden spoon. Take care that it does not boil.

Transfer the curd to a bowl, cover and allow to cool. Then chill for at least 1 hour (or up to 2 days in the refrigerator).

To make the pastry, sift the flour and a pinch of salt into a bowl and rub in the butter and vegetable fat until the mixture resembles crumbs. Add up to 3 tablespoons iced water and work until the dough can be rolled into a ball. Transfer to a floured surface and work until the dough is smooth. Reshape into a ball, cover and chill for 1 hour.

Roll out the dough on a lightly floured surface and cut out 8cm/3¼ in rounds (or 11 x 7.5cm/4½ x 3in rectangles). Use to line 16 fluted round or oval tartlet tins. Prick and chill for 1 hour.

Preheat the oven to 220°C/425°F/Gas Mark 7. Bake the tartlet shells blind for about 15-20 minutes, or until golden. Remove the pastry shells from the tins and allow to cool on a wire rack. (The shells can be made up to 2 days ahead and kept in an airtight container.) Fill each shell with lemon curd and decorate with the sliced fruits.

Candied Watermelon

1 tsp alum powder
  (available from chemists)
2.25kg/5lb peeled
  watermelon seeded and
  cut into 1cm/½ in cubes
450g/1lb caster sugar

1 lemon, sliced
1 x 10cm/4in piece of fresh
  root ginger, peeled and
  thinly sliced
3 cloves
4 mace blades

Makes about 2.25kg/5lb

In a ceramic, glass or enamelled bowl, mix the alum and 1l/1¾ pints water, until the alum is completely dissolved. Add the watermelon cubes and cover. Chill overnight.

Thoroughly drain the watermelon cubes. In a large heavy saucepan, stir together the sugar, sliced lemon, ginger, cloves and mace with 250ml/8fl oz

Fruit-topped lemon curd tartlets.

water. Add the melon cubes and bring the liquid to simmering point, stirring gently to dissolve the sugar. Cook over low heat for 45 minutes. Remove the melon cubes with a slotted spoon to sterilized jars, leaving just enough room for liquid to cover the cubes.

Bring the liquid to the boil and continue to boil until the syrup is thick and reaches 112°C/230°F on a sugar thermometer. Pour the syrup over the watermelon cubes in the jars and seal while still hot. Leave for at least 3 days before using; the cubes will keep for 6 months to 1 year.

Aubergine Sambal with Warm Chapati Strips

450g/1lb aubergine, trimmed	½ tsp crumbled dried red chillis
1 tbsp sunflower oil	Salt
1 small onion, chopped	2 tbsp fresh lime juice
½ green pepper, seeded and chopped	3 tbsp double cream
	3 tbsp chopped fresh parsley
60g/2oz grated fresh coconut	Prepared chapatis, cut into strips
	Groundnut oil, for frying

Makes about 350ml/12fl oz sambal

Preheat the oven to 180°C/350°F/Gas Mark 4. Bake the aubergine for about 1 hour or until soft. Allow to cool.

Heat the sunflower oil in a frying pan and sauté the onion and green pepper until softened and lightly coloured, about 6 minutes.

Cut the aubergine in half lengthways. With a large spoon, scoop the pulp from the aubergine into the bowl of a food processor. Scrape in the fried onion and green pepper, and add coconut, chilli flakes, and salt to taste. Process until thoroughly mixed. With the motor still running, add the lime juice and cream. Process until smooth. Stir in the chopped parsley by hand. Spoon into a decorative bowl and chill, covered, for at least 3 hours (or up to overnight).

Deep fry the chapati strips for 2 minutes and drain on kitchen paper. Serve warm with the chilled sambal.

Italian Antipasto

Think of Italian food and chances are rich tomato sauces, pasta and olives will be among the first ingredients to come to mind. These are certainly included in our menu for an Italian feast, but so are less obvious items like Neapolitan crostini and sardine paste, Genoese pesto and Sicilian caponata. The goat cheese of the Tuscan hills and the corn-based polenta of the northeast serve as inspirations for two more dishes, making this a cook's tour of the peninsula – and even the pasta is finger-friendly!

Italian Market Olives

300g/10oz black or green olives	*¼ tsp black peppercorns*
½ lemon, thinly sliced	*¼ tsp crushed juniper berries*
3 tbsp fresh lemon juice	*1 tsp crumbled dried red chillis*
1 small red onion, halved and thinly sliced	*Extra fine virgin olive oil (about 350ml/12fl oz)*
3 tbsp fresh rosemary	

illustrated on page 91

Makes about 300g/10oz

Bring a saucepan of water to the boil and add the olives. Blanch for 1 minute, then drain thoroughly.

In a glass jar, combine the sliced lemon, lemon juice, onion, rosemary and spices. Add the still-warm olives and stir with a fork to mix well. Pour over enough olive oil to cover, and seal the jar. Shake a few times to mix, then leave in a dark, cool place for at least 5 days, shaking the jar occasionally. (The olives will keep for up to 1 year.)

Drain before serving, but let the seasonings cling to the olives.

Celery with Pesto

90g/3oz mozzarella cheese, grated	*4 tbsp red wine vinegar*
60g/2oz pecorino Romano cheese, grated	*2 tbsp olive oil*
3 tbsp chopped pine kernels	*1 bunch of celery, trimmed*
60g/2oz fresh basil leaves, chopped	*Celery leaves, to garnish*

illustrated on page 91

Makes about 30

Make the pesto filling: in a food processor with a metal blade, combine 60g/2oz of the mozzarella, the pecorino and 2 tablespoons pine kernels and process to a paste. Add the basil leaves and vinegar and blend until combined. With the motor running, gradually add the olive oil and blend until the filling has a thick mayonnaise-like consistency. Stir in the remaining mozzarella. (The filling may be made up to 2 days ahead of time and kept, covered and chilled.)

Cut the celery stalks from the core; trim off the top and bottom ends, and run a sharp knife down the back of each stalk to slice off a layer of ribs, making a flat base. With a knife, spread the filling into the celery stalks. Sprinkle with the remaining chopped pine kernels and cut the stalks diagonally in 5cm/2in lengths. Arrange attractively on a serving platter and garnish with celery leaves.

Clockwise from the top: celery with pesto, crostini with Sicilian sardine paste, caponata-filled tomatoes, fuselli crunchies, Italian market olives.

Scallop, Raddichio and Goat Cheese Bites

225g/8oz mature hard or
  semi-soft goat's cheese
16 large scallops or 32
  queen scallops, cleaned
  without corals
1 small raddichio
8 leaves of oak leaf or Rollo
  Rosso lettuce

Lemon slices, to garnish

Dressing
2 tbsp tarragon vinegar
Salt and black pepper
5 tbsp extra virgin olive oil
2 tbsp chopped fresh
  tarragon

illustrated on page 93

Makes 16

Make the dressing: in a bowl, combine the vinegar and salt and pepper to taste. Beat in the oil in a stream, adding a little tarragon alternately, until the dressing is emulsified and the tarragon completely incorporated.

Cut the goat's cheese into 32 small cubes and toss in the dressing. Leave to marinate for at least 2 hours. (This may be made ahead and left, covered and chilled, for up to 2 days.)

Preheat the grill to high. Brush the scallops with a little of the dressing and grill them until done, about 3-5 minutes, depending on size.

Turn once during cooking, and brush again with the dressing. Cut the large scallops in half. Remove the cheese cubes from the dressing with a slotted spoon (reserving the dressing). Tear the raddichio and lettuce into bite-sized pieces.

Take a small wooden skewer and thread a doubled up ruffle of lettuce on to it. Follow with a scallop (or scallop half), a piece of raddichio, a cube of goat's cheese, more lettuce, more scallop, more raddichio, cheese and lettuce. Repeat with more skewers and the remaining ingredients. Brush some of the dressing over the 'kebabs' and serve, garnished with lemon slices.

Caponata-Filled Tomatoes

20 small Canary tomatoes
3 tbsp olive oil
1 small onion, finely
  chopped
2 garlic cloves, crushed
1 celery stalk, finely diced
½ small red pepper, seeded
  and finely diced
1 small courgette, finely
  diced
½ small aubergine, finely
  diced

Salt and black pepper
60g/2oz canned chopped
  Italian tomatoes
30g/1oz raisins, chopped
1½ tbsp balsamic vinegar
30g/1oz stoned green olives,
  sliced
1 tbsp finely chopped fresh
  flat-leaf parsley
1 tbsp finely chopped fresh
  basil leaves
Shredded frisée, to garnish

illustrated on page 91

Makes 20

Cut the tops from the tomatoes and reserve them. With a spoon, carefully hollow out the tomatoes, discarding the seeds and reserving any flesh. Turn the tomato shells upside-down to drain.

Heat 1 tablespoon of the oil in a frying pan and sauté the onion, garlic and celery until softened and lightly coloured. Reserve in a bowl. Add more oil to the pan and sauté the red pepper and courgette until softened; add to the onion mixture. Add the remaining oil to the pan and sauté the aubergine, a little at a time, until it is softened and browned. Add to the other vegetables. Season to taste.

Put the canned tomatoes, the reserved tomato flesh, the raisins and vinegar into the frying pan. Cook, stirring frequently, until the liquid has almost evaporated. Pour the mixture over the vegetables and stir in the olives, parsley and basil. Cover and leave to cool to room temperature. (This may be made up to 1 day ahead and kept, covered and chilled, with the tomatoes kept separately.)

Spoon a little of the filling into each tomato and replace the tops at an angle. Arrange on a serving plate garnished with frisée.

Garlicky Mixed Tortellini

450g/1 lb mixed coloured
tortellini, either spinach-
or mushroom-filled

Dressing
1 garlic clove, crushed
Salt and black pepper

2 tbsp red wine vinegar
4 tbsp olive oil

To Garnish
Shredded frisée
Watercress
Tomato quarters

illustrated on page 93

Makes about 30

In a large bowl, combine the garlic with salt and
pepper to taste. Mash together, and add the vinegar
until you have a paste. Beat in the oil in a stream,
continuing until emulsified.

Bring a large saucepan of salted water to the boil.
Drop in the tortellini, with a drop of oil. Cook for
about 12-15 minutes, or until tender but not falling
apart. Drain thoroughly.

Add the tortellini to the bowl and toss in the
dressing. Let it absorb the flavour for about 2 hours,
then thread one of each colour tortellini on to
cocktail sticks. Serve at room temperature, garnished with frisée, watercress and tomato.

Left: *garlicky mixed tortellini.*
Right: *scallop, raddichio and goat cheese bites.*

Stuffed Eggs Tonnato

6 hard-boiled eggs
1x 200g/7oz can tuna fish
in oil, drained and flaked
1 tbsp black olive paste
4 tbsp mayonnaise

1 tsp Dijon mustard
½ tsp celery salt
2 tbsp finely chopped spring
onion
Italian pickled peppers

Makes 12

Halve the eggs lengthways; remove the yolks and
reserve the whites. Place the yolks in a bowl and
mash with a fork. Add the tuna, olive paste, mayonnaise, mustard and celery salt and continue to mash
and blend until the mixture is completely combined. Stir in the spring onions. (The filling and
egg whites may be kept, covered and chilled separately, for up to 2 days.)

Fill each of the 12 egg white halves with some of
the tuna fish mixture and decorate with a curled
pickled pepper.

Deep-Fried Polenta Puffs with Spinach Dip

200g/7oz cornmeal for polenta	**Dip**
60g/2oz dry breadcrumbs	150g/5oz frozen chopped spinach, thawed
75g/2½ oz self-raising flour	250ml/8fl oz soured cream
¼ tsp baking powder	120ml/4fl oz mayonnaise
1 tsp caster sugar	½ packet dry onion soup mix
1 egg, beaten	
½ tsp cayenne pepper	3 tbsp chopped fresh parsley
1 tsp Italian mixed herbs	3 spring onions, chopped
2 tbsp soured cream	2 tsp chopped fresh dill
120g/4oz frozen or canned sweetcorn, thawed if necessary and drained	1 tsp Dijon mustard
	1 tsp prepared Italian salad dressing or vinaigrette
Groundnut oil, for deep frying	¼ tsp garlic paste
Red pepper slices, to garnish	2 canned pimientoes, cut into thin 2.5cm/1in strips

illustrated on page 95

**Makes 25 puffs
and 900ml/1½ pints**

Make the dip first. Squeeze the spinach to remove any excess moisture. In the bowl of a food processor or blender, combine all the dip ingredients except the pimientoes. Process until the spinach is chopped and the dip is well combined. Stir in the pimiento strips. Pour the dip into a serving bowl and chill. (The dip can be made up to 1 day ahead and kept, covered and chilled.)

To make the puffs, combine the cornmeal, breadcrumbs, flour, baking powder and sugar in a large bowl. Stir in the egg, cayenne pepper, herbs and soured cream. Add enough water – about 175ml/6fl oz – to make a stiffish dough. Fold in the sweetcorn. (The dough can be made up to 2 hours ahead of time.)

Heat oil in a heavy saucepan or deep-fryer until very hot. Drop in the dough by tablespoons, in batches of 4-5, and fry until they are puffed and golden, about 4 minutes. Remove with a slotted spoon, drain on kitchen paper and keep warm. Repeat with the remaining dough.

Pile the puffs on a serving platter around the bowl of spinach dip and garnish with red pepper.

Fuselli Crunchies

300g/10oz mixed or plain fuselli (pasta twists)	¼ tsp dried oregano
	Pinch of ground rosemary
Groundnut oil, for deep frying	60g/2oz Parmesan cheese, grated
½ tsp dried basil	¼ tsp garlic salt
¼ tsp dried thyme	Pinch of cayenne pepper

illustrated on page 91

Makes about 1.5 l/2½ pints

Bring a large saucepan of salted water to the boil. Add the pasta and a drop of oil, and bring back to the boil. Cook about 8 minutes, or until barely tender. Drain the fuselli, rinse with cold water and drain again thoroughly.

Spread out sheets of kitchen paper and scatter the pasta over them. Pat to dry a little and leave for about 30 minutes, or until it is sticky to the touch. Toss the pasta in 2 tablespoons of oil.

In a deep fryer or saucepan, heat a 2.5cm/1in layer of oil until very hot. Take up a handful of pasta and drop it in the oil, one piece at a time, until there are about 10-12 pieces in the pan. Deep-fry for about 3-4 minutes until lightly coloured, then remove with a slotted spoon to kitchen paper to drain. Repeat with the remaining pasta.

When all has been fried and thoroughly drained, place the pasta in a paper or polythene bag with all the herbs, cheese, garlic salt and cayenne and shake until the fuselli is coated. Leave to cool.

Serve the same day (or store in an airtight container for up to 2 weeks).

Crostini with Sicilian Sardine Paste

Deep-fried polenta puffs with spinach dip.

2x 120g/4oz cans sardines
in oil, drained
60g/2oz ricotta cheese
60g/2oz fontina cheese,
grated
1 tsp fresh lemon juice
2 tbsp drained capers,
chopped
Ground black pepper

Crostini
120g/4oz unsalted butter

1x 120g/4oz can
anchovies, drained and
mashed
2 tbsp finely chopped fresh
parsley
2 tsp fresh lemon juice
24x 5mm/¼ in thick slices
from French baguette

To Garnish
Fresh parsley sprigs
Lemon twists

illustrated on page 91

Makes 24

To make the sardine paste, in a bowl, mash the sardines with a fork. Work in the ricotta, fontina and lemon juice, then stir in the capers and pepper to taste. Reserve. (The paste may be made ahead and kept overnight covered and chilled.)

Preheat the oven to 180°C/350°F/Gas Mark 4.

For the crostini, in a saucepan, melt the butter. Add the mashed anchovies, parsley and lemon juice and beat until combined. Brush each of the bread slices with some of the anchovy mixture, place on greased baking sheets and bake for 10-15 minutes, or until crisp.

Spread a little of the sardine paste in the centre of each of the crostini. Arrange on a serving platter and garnish with parsley and lemon twists.

The Perfect Picnic

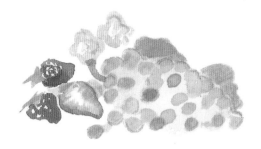

Menu

Avocado and Carrot Squares

Prawn and Cucumber Bowls

Creole Chicken Wings

Tabbouleh in Chicory Cups

Beef and Smoked Ham Cigars

Chocolate-Dipped Fruit

Lemon Squares

Clockwise from the left: *chocolate-dipped fruit, lemon squares, Creole chicken wings, prawn and cucumber bowls, tabbouleh in chicory cups, beef and smoked ham cigars.*

Avocado and Carrot Squares

2 ripe avocados, peeled and stoned	wholemeal bread, crusts removed
1 tsp ground cumin	2 tbsp finely chopped fresh coriander
3 tsp lemon juice	
Salt and black pepper	2 medium carrots, grated
4 tbsp mayonnaise	Fresh coriander sprigs, to garnish
8 slices of toasted	

Makes 16

Chop the avocado flesh into small pieces and place in a bowl. Mash to a creamy paste with the cumin, lemon juice and salt and pepper to taste.

Spread the mayonnaise on the slices of toast. Spread the avocado filling on four of the toast slices. Top each avocado toast with a sprinkling of chopped coriander and grated carrot. Place the other pieces of toast on top, mayonnaise-side down. Cut the sandwiches into four and pile into a picnic container. Garnish with coriander sprigs.

Prawn and Cucumber Bowls

1 cucumber (about 450g/ 1 lb)	1 tsp garlic chilli sauce
90g/3oz peeled cooked prawns, chopped	½ tsp dry mustard
	1 tbsp chopped fresh dill
1 tbsp soured cream	Fresh dill sprigs, to garnish

illustrated on page 97

Makes 10-12

With a sharp knife, cut the cucumber across into 2.5cm/1in thick slices. Use a melon baller to hollow out each slice, leaving a thin shell along the sides and bottom. Turn the 'bowls' upside-down on kitchen paper to drain; discard the seeds and chop the remaining flesh into small pieces. Let that drain thoroughly too.

In a bowl, combine the chopped cucumber, prawns, soured cream, chilli sauce, mustard and chopped dill. Toss lightly together. (The mixture can be made 1 hour ahead and kept chilled.)

Divide the prawn mixture between the cucumber bowls, and gently fill them. Garnish with dill sprigs and pack into a picnic container.

Creole Chicken Wings

900g/2 lb chicken wings (about 12), tips cut off	2 tbsp Worcestershire sauce
2 tbsp sunflower oil	6 tbsp tomato ketchup
2 onions, finely chopped	1 tbsp Tabasco sauce
2 garlic cloves, crushed	1 tbsp smoky barbecue sauce
2 tsp dark brown sugar	1 tsp Dijon mustard
2 tsp chopped fresh thyme	Watercress sprigs, to garnish
1 tbsp malt vinegar	

illustrated on page 97

Makes about 12

Preheat the grill to high. Cook the chicken wings for 10 minutes, turning to brown evenly.

Meanwhile, heat the oil in a frying pan and sauté the onions until softened and lightly coloured. Add the garlic and stir briefly, then stir in the brown sugar, thyme, vinegar, Worcestershire sauce, ketchup, Tabasco, smoky barbecue sauce and mustard. Cook for 5 minutes, stirring.

Transfer the wings to the sauce and cook, covered, for a further 10 minutes, turning once or twice. (The wings can be cooked up to this point earlier in the day and finished just before serving.)

Return the wings to the grill and grill for 3-4 minutes, or until browned. Serve the wings garnished with watercress sprigs. The sauce can be served alongside as a dip, if liked.

Tabbouleh in Chicory Cups

175g/6oz burghul	45g/1½ oz fresh mint, finely chopped
3 tbsp fresh lemon juice	
4 tbsp olive oil	30g/1oz fresh flat-leaf parsley, finely chopped
3 tomatoes, seeded and diced	Pinch of cayenne pepper
½ cucumber, seeded and diced	Salt and black pepper
	16 chicory leaves (about 1 large head)
6 spring onions, finely chopped	Radish roses, to garnish

illustrated on page 97

Makes 16

In a large bowl, soak the burghul in boiling salted water to cover for 1 hour. Drain the burghul and squeeze it dry in a clean tea towel.

Toss the burghul with the lemon juice and oil and leave for 1 hour, then stir in the tomatoes, cucumber, spring onions, mint and parsley. Season to taste and add a pinch of cayenne pepper. (The salad can be kept, covered and chilled, for up to 1 hour before serving.)

Divide the mixture between the chicory leaves and arrange in a sunray pattern on a large plate. Garnish the centre of the plate with radish roses.

Beef and Smoked Ham Cigars

1 Granny Smith apple, peeled, cored and grated	*8 slices of rare beef*
3 tbsp soured cream	*8 thin slices of smoked ham*
1 tbsp prepared horseradish	*Butter, softened*
Salt and black pepper	*4 long slices of pumpernickel bread*
120g/4oz Gruyère cheese, grated	
2 tbsp Dijon mustard	**To Garnish**
1 tbsp caraway seeds	*Endive sprigs*
	Cherry tomatoes

illustrated on page 97

Makes 16

In a small bowl, combine the grated apple, soured cream, prepared horseradish and salt and pepper to taste. (This may be made up to 2 hours ahead and chilled, covered.)

In another small bowl, combine the Gruyère, mustard, mayonnaise and caraway seeds. (This can be made up to 2 hours ahead.)

Trim the beef slices of any fat. Spread out the slices and divide the apple mixture among them, spreading it thinly. Roll up the slices cigar-fashion and set aside.

Trim the ham slices of any fat. Spread out the slices of ham and divide the Gruyère mixture among them. Spread it thinly and roll up the slices cigar-fashion.

Butter the long slices of pumpernickel. Place a 'cigar' on an edge of the bread and trim the bread to fit it. Repeat with the remaining 'cigars'. Arrange attractively, alternating ham and beef. Garnish the plate with endive sprigs and cherry tomatoes.

Chocolate-Dipped Fruit

120g/4oz top-quality bitter chocolate	*segments, strawberries, pineapple slices, pieces of sliced orange with peel, preserved stem ginger*
Assorted small fruits or pieces, e.g. clementine	

illustrated on page 96

Makes 25

Only use firm, dry fruit, never any mushy pieces. The fruit must be eaten the day it is made.

Line a baking sheet with baking parchment. Break the chocolate into a bowl set over a pan of boiled water (but do not let the bowl touch the water). Heat gently for just long enough to melt the chocolate, then remove from the heat. Dip the fruit pieces into the chocolate, covering about half of the fruit. (In the case of strawberries, keep the stalk on and hold it when dipping.) Lay the fruit on the parchment and leave in a cool place until set. Pack carefully in a picnic container.

Lemon Squares

120g/4oz butter, melted	**Topping**
175g/6oz plain flour	*2 eggs*
30g/1oz icing sugar, sifted	*175g/6oz caster sugar*
Icing sugar, to finish	*2 tbsp plain flour*
	½ tsp baking powder
	Grated zest of 1 lemon
	2 tbsp fresh lemon juice

illustrated on page 96

Makes 12

Preheat the oven to 180°C/350°F/Gas Mark 4. Line an 18 x 25cm/7 x 10in Swiss roll tin with baking parchment.

In a bowl, combine the melted butter, flour and sugar; stir until well mixed. Use your hands to spread the mixture in the tin. Bake for 15 minutes.

Meanwhile, put all the topping ingredients into a large bowl and beat together until well mixed. Pour the topping over the half-cooked base in the tin and return it to the oven. Bake for 20-25 minutes, until the topping is set and golden. While still warm, cut into squares. When cool, sprinkle with sifted icing sugar. Pack into a picnic container.

Southeast Asian Delights

While Western palates have long been familiar with Cantonese cooking, and the introduction of Pekinese, Szchewan and other regional cuisines has extended appreciation of that great nation's culinary wealth, the cooking of Thailand, Indonesia and Malaysia has come to our notice far more recently. The characteristic use of fruit in savoury dishes, the flavours of coriander, coconut, lemon and lime (in both fruit and grass), distinguish all three, while the discriminating use of hot pepper or chillies adds a fillip to everything from soup to nuts.

Prawn Crackers

Groundnut oil, for deep frying

225g/8oz prawn wafers from Oriental supermarket

illustrated on page 101

Makes 225g/8oz

Heat the oil in a wok or deep frying pan until very hot. Drop the wafers in one at a time and fry until puffed up, making room for others as they cook. Remove with a slotted spoon to drain on kitchen paper. Test with one or two crackers to find the right temperature for the oil: too cold and they will become sodden and leathery, too hot and they will brown. Adjust the temperature to accommodate. Cool thoroughly before serving or storing. (These will keep up to 1 week in an airtight container.)

Clockwise from the top: prawn crackers, lamb and chicken saté with peanut sauce, stuffed squid packets.

Lamb and Chicken Saté with Peanut Sauce

1 small onion, finely chopped
1 garlic clove, crushed
1 tsp chopped fresh coriander
1 tsp chopped fresh root ginger
1 tbsp rice wine vinegar
1 tbsp sesame oil
1 tsp sambal olek or Chinese chilli paste
225g/8oz lamb fillet
225g/8oz boneless chicken breast

Sauce
½ tsp shrimp paste
60g/2oz unsalted roasted peanuts
3 tbsp chopped spring onion
2 garlic cloves, chopped
1 tbsp groundnut oil
2 tbsp fresh lemon juice
½ tsp sambal olek or Chinese chilli paste
Salt and black pepper

To Garnish
Lemon wedges
Fresh coriander sprigs

illustrated on page 101

Makes about 20

In a deep bowl, combine the onion, garlic, coriander, ginger, vinegar, oil and sambal olek. Stir well to mix. With a sharp knife, cut the lamb and chicken into 10-12.5cm/4-5in long, thin slices. Flatten and pound with a mallet, if desired. Drop the slices into the onion and herb mixture and stir to coat. Cover the bowl tightly and chill overnight.

Make the sauce: in the bowl of a food processor or blender, combine the shrimp paste, peanuts, spring onion and garlic. Process until finely chopped. Heat the oil in a saucepan and when it is just hot, add the peanut mixture. Sauté for 1 minute, or until it is thick. Stir in the lemon juice, sambal olek and seasoning to taste. Scrape into a bowl and reserve.

Preheat the grill to high. Thread each long slice of lamb and chicken onto a short wooden skewer and grill in batches for about 6 minutes, turning once. Serve warm, ranged round the peanut sauce and garnished with lemon wedges and coriander.

Beef Dumplings with Mango Dip

450g/1 lb lean minced beef
1 small onion, finely
  chopped
1 tbsp sunflower oil
2 tsp crushed garlic
2 tsp finely chopped fresh
  root ginger
½ tsp ground turmeric
½ tsp cumin seeds
¼ tsp cayenne pepper
Salt and black pepper
30-35 frozen won ton
  wrappers, thawed (1 packet)

1 tbsp sesame oil
1 tbsp red wine vinegar
1 tsp soy sauce

Dip
3 tbsp mango chutney
3 tbsp fresh lime juice
1 tsp curry powder
6 tbsp mayonnaise
4 tbsp plain yogurt
Paprika

illustrated on page 103

Makes 30-35

In a food processor, blend together all the ingredients for the dip. Put in a decorative bowl, cover and chill until needed. (The sauce can be made up to 2 days ahead of time and kept covered and chilled.)

In a frying pan, sauté the meat until it is browned and crumbly. Drain the meat and transfer to a bowl. In the same frying pan, sauté the onion in the oil until softened and coloured. Stir in the garlic, ginger, spices and seasoning to taste, and cook for about 2 minutes. Scrape the onion mixture into the meat and toss together.

Lay 6 won ton wrappers on the work surface. Place 1-2 teaspoons of beef filling on each, moisten the edges of the wrappers and fold each over to form a triangle, pinching to seal well. Repeat with the remaining meat and wrappers. (The prepared won tons can be kept, covered and chilled, for up to 2 days.)

Bring a large pan of water to the boil and drop in the triangles a few at a time. Cook for about 5 minutes each, carefully turning over once. Lift out with a slotted spoon.

In a bowl, whisk together the sesame oil, vinegar and soy sauce. Gently toss the won tons in the vinegar coating. Pile the won tons on a platter and serve while still warm with the mango dip, sprinkled with a little paprika.

Stuffed Squid Packets

30g/1oz dried Chinese
  mushrooms
60g/2oz transparent rice
  noodles
6 canned water chestnuts,
  drained
175g/6oz minced pork
1 garlic clove, crushed
4 spring onions, chopped

1 tbsp oriental fish sauce
Salt and black pepper
16-20 baby squid, well
  cleaned, with tentacles
  reserved
Groundnut oil
Watercress, chopped
Lime slices, to garnish

illustrated on page 101

Makes about 16-20

In a bowl, soak the mushrooms in hot water to cover for 30 minutes. In another bowl, soak the rice noodles in hot water to cover for 25 minutes. Remove the mushrooms, squeeze out excess moisture and chop. Remove the noodles, squeeze out excess moisture and chop. Put these and the water chestnuts in the bowl of a food processor with a metal blade. Process until finely chopped. Add the pork, garlic, spring onions and fish sauce. Process until well combined. Season the mixture to taste with salt and pepper.

Rinse and drain the squid bodies. Finely chop the tentacles and add to the meat mixture. Pat the bodies dry and divide the meat mixture among them. (The squid may be stuffed a few hours ahead of time and kept, covered and chilled.)

Secure the openings with cocktail sticks. Heat about 2 tablespoons of oil in a frying pan and sauté half the stuffed squid over medium-low heat for about 4 minutes. Prick the squid with a cocktail stick, raise the heat slightly, and continue cooking for about another 5 minutes, turning gently. Lift out with a slotted spoon on to kitchen paper to drain, then keep warm while cooking the remaining squid in the same way, adding a little more oil to the pan if necessary.

Allow to cool slightly, then remove the cocktail sticks and serve warm or at room temperature on a bed of watercress and garnished with lime slices.

Spiced Baby Sweetcorn

Beef dumplings with mango dip.

1½ tsp soy sauce
2 tbsp fresh lemon juice
½ tsp crumbled dried red
  chillis
2 tsp sesame oil

1 garlic clove, finely chopped
1 tbsp finely chopped fresh
  coriander
20-25 baby sweetcorn
1 tbsp groundnut oil

Makes 20-25

Combine the soy sauce, lemon juice, chillies, sesame oil, garlic and coriander in a bowl. Add the baby sweetcorn and toss to coat. Leave to marinate for 1-2 hours, tossing occasionally.

In a frying pan, heat the groundnut oil. Remove the sweetcorn from the marinade and cook over medium heat for about 10 minutes, stirring to cook evenly. Drain the sweetcorn on kitchen paper, drizzle with a little of the marinade, and serve.

Sunshine Mix

120ml/4fl oz sunflower oil
2 tsp curry powder
½ tsp dried shrimp paste
120g/4oz raisins
120g/4oz shelled peanuts

90g/3oz dried banana
  chips
90g/3oz sunflower seeds
Salt

Makes about 450g/1 lb

In a large frying pan over medium-high heat, stir together the oil, curry powder and shrimp paste, pressing the paste to crush and spread it. Cook until the curry powder begins to colour. Add the raisins and cook, stirring, until puffed, about 1 minute. Add the peanuts, banana chips and sunflower seeds and stir until coated and heated.

Scrape on to kitchen paper to drain and pat with more paper. Sprinkle with salt to taste and serve warm or at room temperature. (This will keep in an airtight container for up to 1 week.)

Banana Lime Tarts

175g/6oz digestive biscuits, crushed
150g/5oz blanched almonds, toasted and ground
120g/4oz unsalted butter, melted
120g/4oz soft light brown sugar
Lime twists, to decorate

Filling
3 size-2 eggs, separated
400ml/14fl oz canned condensed milk
120ml/4fl oz fresh lime juice
2-3 small bananas
75g/2½ oz caster sugar

illustrated on page 105

Makes 10-12

Preheat the oven to 180°C/350°F/Gas Mark 4. In a bowl, mix together the digestive biscuits, ground almonds, melted butter and brown sugar until well combined. Press the mixture over the bottom and up the sides of 10-12 loose-bottomed tartlet tins, each 7.5-8.5cm/3-3¼in in diameter. Bake on the middle shelf of the oven for about 12 minutes, or until browned lightly. Cool in the tins on a wire rack, then carefully ease out of the tins and place on baking sheets.

Meanwhile, beat the egg yolks with the condensed milk, and stir in the lime juice slowly until combined. Slice the bananas and divide the slices between each of the tartlet shells. Spoon the egg yolk mixture on top of the banana slices and chill for about 1 hour.

In a bowl, beat the egg whites to soft peaks, then beat in the sugar a tablespoon at a time until the meringue is stiff. Spread the meringue over the filled tartlets, swirling decoratively.

Bake the tartlets at the same heat for 15 minutes, or until the meringue is touched with gold. Chill for at least 2 hours before removing from the baking sheets and serving. Decorate with twists of lime. (The tartlets may be made a day ahead of time and kept chilled.)

Vegetable Lettuce Rolls

450g/1 lb mushrooms
30g/1oz unsalted butter
1 small red pepper, seeded and finely chopped
1 courgette, finely chopped
1 carrot, grated
2 spring onions, finely chopped

225g/8oz cream cheese, at room temperature
1 tbsp chopped fresh coriander
Salt and black pepper
1 tsp garlic paste
2 tbsp dry Sherry
2 Webb's Wonder or iceberg lettuces

Makes 30

Chop the mushrooms roughly and put into the bowl of a food processor with a metal blade. Add 450ml/¾ pint water and process until the mushrooms are finely chopped. Pour the mixture into a saucepan, bring to the boil and leave to simmer for 30 minutes.

Meanwhile, heat the butter in a frying pan and saute the red pepper, courgette, carrot and spring onions until softened. Transfer the vegetables to a bowl and allow to cool.

Drain the mushrooms, reserving the liquid, and add them to the sautéed vegetables. Return the mushroom liquid to the saucepan and boil until it is reduced to about 3 tablespoons; cool.

Add the cream cheese, coriander, seasoning to taste, garlic paste and Sherry to the vegetables in the bowl. Stir to combine, then add the cooled mushroom liquid and mix well. Cover and chill. (This mixture can be made ahead and kept, covered and chilled, for up to 4 days.)

Separate out 30 lettuce leaves, which should be at least 12.5x10cm/5x4in. Bring a saucepan of water to the boil and drop in the leaves; drain immediately and run the leaves under cold water. Pat dry with kitchen paper. Trim the leaves of tough ribs and tears.

Top each leaf with some of the vegetable mixture and form into a compact roll, tucking in the sides. Chill for no more than 2 hours before using.

Left: *lychee-pineapple bites.* Right: *banana lime tarts.*

Lychee-Pineapple Bites

3x 400g/14oz cans of   cheese, grated
  stoned lychees, drained   1x 400g/14oz can
60g/2oz mature Cheddar   pineapple pieces, drained

---

illustrated on page 105

Makes 24

Gently open the holes left by the lychee stone. Stuff with a fingerful of grated cheese and a pineapple piece. Secure with a cocktail stick. Serve the stuffed lychees in decorative bowls.

Afro-Carib Tastees

The Caribbean Islands vary greatly in their resources. A few are able to grow a wide variety of fruit, but most import. Fish is plentiful but generally expensive; some islands have a flavourful industry in harvesting spices. Jamaica raises allspice, Granada nutmeg, while other spices are grown in scattered profusion. Popular imports are the staples of Africa and the Southern United States – avocado, sweet potato, coconut, peanuts and greens – which are seasoned with the influence of the immigrant settlers; the cheeses of the Dutch Antilles, the cod and jerky brought by generations of British and other mariners.

Buttered Brazil Chips

175g/6oz shelled Brazil nuts

45g/1½ oz butter, melted
Salt

illustrated on page 107

Makes about 175g/6oz

In a saucepan, cover the nuts with water and bring to the boil. Boil for 3 minutes, then drain. Allow the nuts to cool, then with a sharp knife, cut the nuts into lengthways chips or slices.

Preheat the oven to 180°C/350°F/Gas Mark 4. Place the chips in a single layer on a baking sheet and brush with the butter. Sprinkle with salt to taste. Bake for about 15 minutes, flipping the chips with a palette knife once or twice, or until the chips are golden. Cool on kitchen paper and pat off excess butter. Serve when dry, or pack into an air-tight jar to keep for up to 2 weeks.

Caribbean Jerky

1x 900g/2 lb piece rump steak
120ml/4fl oz soy sauce
1 tbsp coarse salt
60g/2oz light brown sugar
4 garlic cloves, crushed
2 tbsp ground ginger

1 tbsp ground cinnamon
½ tsp crumbled dried red chillies
Fresh flat-leaf parsley or coriander sprigs, to garnish

illustrated on page 107

Makes about 450g/1 lb

Trim off all fat from the meat. Cut the steak in half along its length. Mix together all the other ingredients in a bowl; immerse the steak pieces and rub thoroughly with the spice mixture. Cover and chill overnight.

Preheat the oven to 85°C/185°F/Gas Mark Low. Lift the meat from the bowl (do not pierce it with a fork) and place directly on the oven racks, over a large baking tray to catch drippings. Bake for about 9-10 hours, or until the meat is firm and dry. (Test by cutting into the centre of the meat; it should be consistently cooked, though with a moister 'feel' than commercial jerky.)

Cool the meat, then slice into thin strips across the grain. Serve garnished with flat-leaf parsley or coriander sprigs. (The jerky will keep, unsliced and wrapped tightly, for up to 1 week, chilled.)

Clockwise from the top: *egg and bacon bundles, beef, coconut and peanut grills, Caribbean jerky, buttered Brazil chips.*

106

Beef, Coconut and Peanut Grills

1 tsp creamed coconut
225g/8oz lean minced beef
1 tbsp fresh lime juice
Salt and black pepper
Pinch of chilli powder
1 pickled jalapeño pepper,
  finely chopped
1 tbsp finely chopped spring
  onion
Large pinch of brown sugar
1 tsp oyster sauce

1 tsp grated fresh root
  ginger
2 tbsp chopped fresh
  coriander
60g/2oz unsalted peanuts,
  finely chopped
60g/2oz sultanas, plumped
  in hot water and drained
30x 5cm/2in rounds of
  wholemeal bread, toasted
Pickled chilli peppers, to
  serve

illustrated on page 107

Makes 30

In a bowl, combine the creamed coconut with 1 tablespoon boiling water and mash together. Stir in the beef and the rest of the ingredients, except the toast and pickled peppers. Work until thoroughly combined. (This can be made up to 1 day ahead and kept covered and chilled.)

Preheat the grill to high. Spread some of the meat mixture on each of the toast rounds and place on a baking sheet. Grill for about 4 minutes, or until the meat mixture is medium rare. Serve warm with the pickled chilli peppers.

Egg and Bacon Bundles

675g/1½ lb chard or kale,
  washed and stalks
  removed
4 hard-boiled eggs
7 streaky bacon rashers,

rind removed, fried and
  finely chopped
Salt and black pepper
150ml/¼ pint olive oil
4 tbsp fresh lemon juice

illustrated on page 107

Makes 20

Cook the chard or kale leaves in a large saucepan of boiling water for about 3 minutes, or until limp. Drain thoroughly. Reserve 20 large leaf halves and chop the remainder finely. Squeeze out the excess moisture from the chopped leaves.

Reserve half a hard-boiled egg, and finely chop the rest. In a bowl, mix together the chopped leaves, eggs and bacon. Season to taste with salt and pepper. Wrap a portion of this filling in each whole leaf and carefully roll up. Arrange attractively on a serving platter. Mix together the oil and lemon juice, drizzle over the bundles, cover tightly and leave for at least 1-2 hours before serving. Garnish with the sieved yolk and chopped white of the reserved egg.

Deep-Fried Banana Kebabs with Lemon Sauce

90g/3oz fresh breadcrumbs
90g/3oz desiccated coconut
90g/3oz caster sugar
1½ tsp ground cinnamon
2 size-4 eggs
Groundnut oil, for deep
  frying
6 large bananas, cut into
  4cm/1½in chunks

Sauce
60g/2oz butter
120g/4oz caster sugar
Grated zest and juice of 1
  lemon
4 tbsp golden syrup

Makes about 12

Make the sauce: melt the butter over low heat and stir in the sugar, lemon zest and juice and the golden syrup. Heat for 5 minutes or until combined. Keep warm.

In a bowl, mix together the breadcrumbs, coconut, sugar and cinnamon. In a small shallow bowl, beat the eggs. Heat oil in a deep fryer or heavy saucepan.

Thread the banana pieces on to 12 small wooden skewers. Dip each first into the egg mixture and then into the breadcrumb mixture. Drop into the hot oil, 3 skewers at a time, and deep fry until golden. Lift out with a slotted spoon, drain on kitchen paper and keep warm while repeating with the remaining banana skewers.

Serve with the warm lemon sauce in a bowl.

Aruba Salt Cod Cakes with Avocado

Left: *pineapple muffins with Jamaican pork.*
Right: *Nevis fruit bakes.*

675g/1½ lb salt cod, soaked overnight in cold water and squeezed dry
175g/6oz mature Gouda cheese, grated
3 tbsp finely chopped fresh parsley
1 tsp dried oregano
½ tsp ground cumin
3 garlic cloves, finely chopped

90g/3oz dried breadcrumbs
4 spring onions, finely chopped
2 eggs, beaten
120ml/4fl oz whipping cream
Groundnut oil, for frying
2 large ripe avocados
2 tbsp fresh lime juice
Salt
Quartered limes, to serve

Makes 16

Flake the salt cod into a bowl. Add the cheese, parsley, oregano, cumin, breadcrumbs, spring onions, eggs and cream and mix, first with a fork and then with the hands. (This mixture may be made ahead and chilled, covered, overnight.)

In a large frying pan, heat 2 tablespoons oil. Take 2 tablespoons of the fish mixture, place in the pan and flatten into a thin patty. Repeat with further cakes, but do not over-crowd. Fry the cakes on both sides and keep warm.

Cut the avocados in half, scrape the flesh into a bowl and add the lime juice and salt to taste. Mash together well. Spoon into a decorative bowl. Serve the cod cakes with the avocado paste and limes.

Pineapple Muffins with Jamaica Pork

225g/8oz canned crushed
  pineapple in juice
Milk
225g/8oz plain flour
60g/2oz caster sugar
1 tbsp baking powder
Salt
¼ tsp grated nutmeg
1 egg, beaten
2 tsp grated orange zest
60g/2oz butter, melted
Butter, softened, to serve

Thin orange wedges, to
  garnish

Pork Filling
2 tbsp whole allspice
3 spring onions, chopped
2 fresh green chilli peppers
¼ tsp ground cinnamon
½ tsp grated nutmeg
Salt and black pepper
1x 325g/11oz pork fillet

illustrated on page 109

Makes 12

First make the pork filling: in a blender, combine all the filling ingredients except the meat. Process until you have a paste, adding a touch of water, if necessary. Rub the paste over the pork and leave it for 2 hours.

Preheat the grill to low. Grill the pork fillet, turning on all sides, until cooked through, about 30 minutes. Cut into thin diagonal slices and reserve.

To make the muffins, drain the pineapple juice into a measuring jug. Add enough milk to make 250ml/8fl oz. In a large bowl, combine the flour, sugar, baking powder, salt to taste and nutmeg. Beat in the juice and milk mixture, the egg, orange zest and melted butter. When the mixture is smooth, stir in the crushed pineapple.

Preheat the oven to 200°C/400°F/Gas Mark 6. Spoon the batter into a greased 12-hole deep muffin tin. Bake for about 20-25 minutes, or until golden and firm to the touch. Allow to cool for about 5 minutes, then remove the muffins from the tin. Split almost through, butter generously, and layer with some of the pork. Serve warm, with thin orange wedges.

Jamaican Crab Dip with Sweet Potato Crisps

675g/1½ lb sweet potatoes,
  peeled
Vegetable oil, for deep frying
Sea salt

Dip
90g/3oz cream cheese,
  softened

120ml/4fl oz mayonnaise
175g/6oz cooked white crab
  meat
60g/2oz red onion, finely
  chopped
1 tbsp fresh lemon juice
¼ tsp Jamaican hot pepper
  sauce

illustrated on page 111

**Makes 675g/1½ lb crisps
and 500ml/16fl oz dip**

First make the sweet potato crisps: with a very sharp knife or a mandoline, cut the sweet potatoes into thin slices. Dry with kitchen paper. Heat oil for deep frying to about 182°C/380°F. Drop in the crisps, in batches, and fry until golden. Remove with a slotted spoon to kitchen paper to drain. Keep warm, or allow to cool to room temperature. Sprinkle the crisps with the salt.

To make the dip, in a heavy saucepan, beat the cream cheese until smooth. Stir in the mayonnaise, then the crab meat, onion, lemon juice and hot pepper sauce. Cook over medium-high heat for 15 minutes, stirring, until bubbly.

Serve the dip in a bowl accompanied by the warm or room-temperature sweet potato crisps.

Jamaican crab dip with sweet potato crisps.

Cheese-and-Mango Biscuits

120g/4oz plain flour	*½ tsp ground ginger*
120g/4oz mature Cheddar	*1 size-2 egg*
cheese, grated	*3-4 tbsp mango chutney*
60g/2oz butter	

Makes 16-18

In the bowl of a food processor fitted with a metal blade, put the flour and Cheddar cheese. Cut in the butter and add the ginger. Process until the mixture resembles breadcrumbs. Add the egg and process until a ball of dough forms around the blade.

Shape the ball into a 4cm/1½in diameter log, wrap tightly and chill for at least 1 hour.

Preheat the oven to 220°C/425°F/Gas mark 7. Slice the log into 16-18 equal rounds and lay on a large ungreased baking sheet, at least 1cm/½in apart. In the centre of each round, make a dent with your thumb and fill with ½ teaspoon chutney.

Bake the biscuits for 14-16 minutes, or until golden. Cool on a wire rack, and either serve warm or at room temperature.

Nevis Fruit Bakes

120g/4oz cottage cheese	*1 small papaya or mango,*
120g/4oz cream cheese	*peeled, seeded and*
½ tsp curry powder	*chopped*
1 tbsp mango chutney	*1 tsp ground cinnamon*
1 tbsp chopped dates	*1 tsp caster sugar*
5 slices of pumpernickel	*10g/½oz butter, melted*
bread, cut into quarters	

---

illustrated on page 109

Makes 20

Preheat the oven to 220°C/425°F/Gas Mark 7. In a bowl, beat together the two cheeses, curry powder, chutney and dates. Lay out the pumpernickel quarters and divide the chopped papaya or mango among them. Top with the cheese mixture. Mix the cinnamon and sugar and sprinkle over the cheese. Drizzle over the butter. Bake for about 10 minutes, until hot and slightly puffed. Serve warm.

A *Children's Party*

Menu

Biscuit-Cutter Sandwiches

Frankfurter Boats

Quick Child-Size Pizzas

Peanut butter and Chocolate Bars

Piggy Back Potatoes

Old-Fashioned Potato Doughnuts

Clockwise from top left: *quick child-size pizzas, frankfurter boats, old-fashioned potato doughnuts, piggy-back potatoes, biscuit-cutter sandwiches, peanut butter and chocolate bars.*

Biscuit-Cutter Sandwiches

16 slices of white bread
16 slices of wholemeal
bread
Butter, softened
2 small crisp apples,
peeled, cored and grated
2 celery stalks, trimmed
and finely chopped

175g/6oz Cheddar cheese,
grated
3 bananas, peeled and
sliced
6 tbsp orange marmalade
Finely chopped fresh parsley
(optional)
Crushed mixed nuts
(optional)

illustrated on page 113

Makes 32

Use biscuit cutters in amusing shapes – hearts, Christmas trees, animals, whatever is seasonal or appropriate. Cut two small shapes from each slice of bread, making sure that you always have a pair of each shape to make a complete sandwich. The white bread will be used for one filling, the wholemeal for the other.

Spread the softened butter thinly on all the white and brown bread shapes. In a bowl, mix together 60g/2oz softened butter with the apples, celery and Cheddar cheese, mashing and stirring to combine. Spread the mixture on 16 of the white bread shapes and cover with the matching shapes.

Lay out 16 wholemeal bread shapes and divide the banana slices among them. Spread the orange marmalade on the other 16 buttered shapes and put the two matching shapes together. (If made well ahead of time, keep the sandwiches tightly covered.)

As an optional finishing touch: on one plate put a thick layer of finely chopped parsley, on another plate crushed nuts. Thinly butter the outsides or edges of the white bread sandwiches and dip into the parsley to coat. Butter the edges of the wholemeal sandwiches and roll in the chopped nuts. Pile attractively on a plate for serving.

Frankfurter Boats

12 American-style
frankfurters
6 processed Cheddar cheese
slices
72 potato sticks
Mustard in a plastic
squeeze bottle

24 mini-gherkins, cut in
half horizontally
12 hot dog buns or finger
rolls
Lettuce
Tomato ketchup

illustrated on page 113

Makes 12

Cook the frankfurters according to packet directions until heated through. Meanwhile, cut the 6 slices of cheese in half diagonally, and thread on to cocktail sticks to resemble sails.

When the frankfurters are cooked, drain them. Cut a slit down the length of each frankfurter. Make 3 small slits down each side of a frank and insert 6 potato stick 'oars' into them. Squeeze a ribbon of mustard down each lengthways slit and place 4 gherkin halves – the 'crew' – down the centre. Finally mount the cheese 'sails' on the 'boats', and sail them on a sea of lettuce. Serve with a pile of toasted buns and additional mustard and ketchup.

Quick Child-Size Pizzas

6 muffins
150ml/ ¼ pint herb tomato
sauce
1 small green pepper,
seeded and thinly sliced
1 onion, thinly sliced

175g/6oz Gruyère or
Cheddar cheese, grated
60g/2oz Parmesan cheese,
grated
4 tbsp sliced stoned black
olives

illustrated on page 112

Makes 12

Preheat the grill to high. Halve the muffins and grill them on a baking sheet for 2-3 minutes on each side, until lightly toasted. Spread the tomato sauce over the cut sides of the muffin halves and top each with some green pepper, onion and Gruyère cheese. Sprinkle over the Parmesan cheese and scatter a few olive rounds on top. Return to the grill and cook for about 5 minutes, until the cheese begins to brown. Serve hot.

Peanut Butter and Chocolate Bars

225g/8oz plain flour
175g/6oz rolled oats
350g/12oz light brown
  sugar
60g/2oz stoned dates,
  chopped

90g/3oz unsalted peanuts,
  chopped
175g/6oz butter, melted
300g/10oz creamy peanut
  butter, softened over heat
120g/4oz plain chocolate

illustrated on page 113

Makes about 25

Preheat the oven to 180°C/350°F/Gas Mark 4.

In a food processor with a metal blade, combine the flour, oats, sugar, dates and peanuts; process to mix and chop. Then add the melted butter through the tube, mixing until you get a gritty dough. (Process in batches, if necessary.) Press the dough evenly into a greased 24 x 34cm/9½ x 13½in baking tin.

Bake until the edges are lightly browned and the biscuit cake is firm in the centre, about 20 minutes (the bars will be chewy). Cut into thirds lengthways, and into 8 or 9 slices crossways. Allow the bars to cool slightly in the tin before removing with a palette knife.

Gently spread the warm bars with the softened peanut butter. Melt the chocolate in a bowl over hot water and drizzle or pipe on to the bars in a decorative pattern. Let the chocolate harden before serving. (The bars will keep in an airtight tin for about 3 days.)

Piggy Back Potatoes

24 small new potatoes
  (about 675g/1½ lb)
12 rashers of streaky
  bacon, rinds removed, cut

in half
2 tsp Dijon mustard
Paprika

illustrated on page 113

Makes 12

Scrub the potatoes and place them in a large saucepan of salted water. Bring to the boil and cook for about 15 minutes or until tender. Drain.

Spread the bacon pieces with a little of the mustard and wrap each round a potato. Dust the exposed potato with a little paprika. Spear pairs of bacon-wrapped potatoes on small wooden skewers. (These can be prepared up to this point ahead of time and kept, covered and chilled, for several hours.)

Preheat the grill to high. Cook the potatoes, turning twice, until they are warmed and the bacon is sizzling. Serve warm.

Old-Fashioned Potato Doughnuts

120g/4oz plain flour
2 tsp baking powder
30g/1oz caster sugar
175g/6oz butter
2 medium potatoes, boiled
  and mashed finely

2 eggs, beaten
1 tsp ground cinnamon
1 tbsp milk
4 tbsp raspberry jam
Oil, for deep frying

illustrated on page 113

Makes about 10-12

Sift the flour and baking powder into a bowl. Add the sugar and rub in the butter until the mixture resembles breadcrumbs. Work in the mashed potatoes, 1 tablespoon at a time, until you have added 8 tablespoons of potato. The dough should be stiff. Stir in the eggs, cinnamon and milk.

Form the dough into a ball, then roll or pat it out on a floured surface until about 1cm/⅛in thick. Cut out rounds with a glass or biscuit cutter. In the centre of each round, place a teaspoon of jam, and form the dough round it into a ball, pinching to make it airtight.

Heat oil for deep frying and drop in 3-4 doughnuts at a time. Cook, turning occasionally, for about 10 minutes, or until golden brown. As they are done, lift out the doughnuts with a slotted spoon, drain on kitchen paper and cool on a wire rack. When cooled, dust with sifted icing sugar. Pile on a plate and serve as fresh as possible. (Children love watching these being made, too!)

American Snacks

Americans have long favoured finger food – look at the success of the hamburger, the hot dog, corn on the cob, French fries and onion rings, among a myriad of other inventions and adaptations. They are all meant to be enjoyed with the minimum of fuss and the maximum of pleasure – never mind the mess, that's why paper napkins are an American institution. This selection of All-American snacks has choices elegant and easy-going, ranging from the luxurious Individual Oysters Rockefeller, to simple Southwestern Corn Muffins with Chilli, to tasty reminders of the Wild West – Potato Skins with Soured Cream, and sweet Maine Blueberry Chewies to finish an American feast!

Citrus Mixed Lettuce Cups

2 tbsp fresh lemon juice
1 tbsp fresh orange juice
Salt and black pepper
4 tbsp olive oil
Dash of Tabasco sauce
120g/4oz mixed oak leaf lettuce, mâche, frisée,
Webb's Wonder lettuce and/or watercress, finely chopped
16 raddichio leaves
90g/3oz Camembert, rind removed, grated
Thinly sliced radish

---

illustrated on page 119

Serves 16

Make the dressing: in a bowl, combine the lemon and orange juices with salt and pepper to taste. Whisk in the oil until emulsified, then stir in the Tabasco. Reserve.

In a large bowl, mix together the various green leaves. Toss with dressing.

Divide the dressed leaves among the raddichio leaves and top each with a little grated Camembert and radish. Arrange on a serving platter.

Spicy Peanut Spread

175g/6oz smooth peanut butter
175ml/6fl oz plain Greek-style yogurt
1 garlic clove, finely chopped
1 pickled jalapeño pepper, finely chopped
Pinch of cayenne pepper
Dry-roasted peanuts
Paprika

To serve
Savoury biscuits
Celery sticks
Dried banana chips

---

illustrated on page 117

Makes about 250ml/8fl oz

In the bowl of a blender or food processor with a metal blade, combine the peanut butter, yogurt, and garlic. Add jalapeño pepper and cayenne to taste. Process until smooth.

Scrape the spread into a decorative bowl and sprinkle with chopped dry-roasted peanuts and paprika. Serve surrounded by savoury biscuits, celery sticks and banana chips to dip into it. (The spread can be made up to 2 days ahead and kept, covered and chilled.)

Clockwise from the top: *Southwestern corn muffins with chilli, potato skins and soured cream, spicy peanut spread, individual oysters Rockefeller.*

Vegetable Balls with Sweet Tomato Dip

60g/2oz green pepper,
  seeded and finely chopped
1 onion, finely chopped
30g/1oz unsalted butter
450g/1 lb courgettes, finely
  grated
2 large carrots, grated
½ tsp ground cumin
2 size-2 eggs
4 tbsp milk
Salt and black pepper
120g/4oz fresh
  breadcrumbs

Dry breadcrumbs, for
  coating
Groundnut oil, for deep
  frying

Tomato Dip
1 small onion, chopped
½ red pepper, seeded and
  chopped
1 tbsp sunflower oil
1 garlic clove, crushed
3 tbsp tomato purée
250ml/8fl oz mayonnaise

illustrated on page 119

Makes about 25

First make the dip: in a saucepan over medium heat, sauté the onion and red pepper in the oil until they are softened, about 8 minutes. Add the garlic and cook for 2 minutes longer. Stir in the tomato purée. Allow to cool, then turn into a food processor or blender and add the mayonnaise. Process until combined and smooth. Scrape into a serving bowl and chill.

To make the vegetable balls, in a saucepan cook the green pepper and onion in the butter until they are softened. Take off the heat and stir in the courgettes, carrots and cumin. Reserve.

In a bowl, beat together the eggs, milk and salt and pepper to taste. Stir in the fresh breadcrumbs, then the courgette mixture. Mix well.

Scoop out tablespoonfuls of the mixture, form into balls and coat in the dry breadcrumbs. Heat oil for deep frying until very hot. Add the balls in batches and fry for about 4-5 minutes or until golden. Drain the balls on kitchen paper and keep warm until they are all cooked. (The balls can be made ahead of time and kept, covered and chilled, for up to 2 days. Reheat in a moderate oven for about 20 minutes before serving.)

Arrange the balls with the bowl of tomato dip and serve.

Miniature Reuben Sandwiches

250g/9oz pastrami or salt
  beef
90g/3oz butter
1 large onion, finely
  chopped
350g/12oz sauerkraut,
  rinsed and drained

16 slices of volksbrot or
  light rye bread
8 slices of Gruyère cheese

To Garnish
Gherkin spears
1 red onion, cut into rings

Makes 32

Thinly slice the pastrami or salt beef. In a large frying pan, melt 30g/1oz of the butter and sauté the onion until softened and lightly coloured. Stir in the sauerkraut and cook until combined and heated thoroughly.

Lay out 8 slices of the bread on a work surface. Divide the sauerkraut between them, then top each with some of the meat and a slice of cheese. Cover with the remaining slices of bread. Cut each sandwich into 4 fingers.

Using the rest of the butter, sauté the small sandwiches in batches until they are lightly browned on both sides and the cheese is melting. Arrange the Reubens attractively on a platter and garnish with gherkin spears and onion rings.

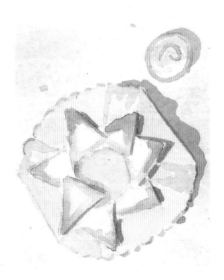

Potato Skins and Soured Cream

Left: *citrus mixed lettuce cups.*
Right: *vegetable balls with sweet tomato dip.*

6 large baking potatoes,
  scrubbed and rubbed with
  olive oil
4-6 tbsp olive oil

1-2 tsp dry mustard
1 tsp sweet paprika
Coarse sea salt
150ml/¼ pint soured cream

illustrated on page 117

Makes about 60 strips

Preheat the oven to 220°C/425°F/Gas Mark 7. Prick the potatoes and bake until done, about 1 hour. When cool, halve them, scoop out the flesh, leaving a thin layer of potato next to the skin, and cut the skins into 5 long strips. In a bowl, mix together the oil, mustard and paprika and brush the strips of skin with the mixture. Lay the strips on a baking tray skin-side up and bake for a further 20 minutes until crisp and brown. Sprinkle with the salt and serve hot with soured cream.

Southwestern Corn Muffins with Chilli

175g/6oz plain flour	Chopped spring onion
175g/6oz fine cornmeal	
2 tsp bicarbonate of soda	**Chilli**
½ tsp baking powder	1 tbsp sunflower oil
1 tsp salt	450g/1 lb minced beef
1 tsp caster sugar	1 garlic clove, finely
60g/2oz butter, melted	chopped
250ml/8fl oz buttermilk	90g/3oz bottled Mexican
3 fresh green chilli peppers,	salsa or taco sauce
seeded and finely chopped	150ml/¼ pint tomato sauce
60g/2oz Cheddar cheese,	2 tbsp dry Mexican chilli
finely grated	seasoning
2 size-2 eggs, beaten	Salt and black pepper

illustrated on page 117

Makes about 30

Make the chilli first: heat the oil in a frying pan and sauté the beef and garlic until the meat is well browned. Stir in the salsa, tomato sauce, chilli seasoning and salt and pepper to taste. Cook for about 10-15 minutes, stirring occasionally. Reserve. (This may be made ahead and kept, covered and chilled, for up to 3 days. Heat through before using.)

To make the muffins, preheat the oven to 220°C/425°F/Gas Mark 7. In a bowl, mix together the flour, cornmeal, bicarbonate of soda, baking powder, salt and sugar. Stir in the butter, buttermilk, chilli peppers, cheese and eggs, mixing to combine thoroughly.

Spoon tablespoons of the batter into buttered bun tins and bake in batches for about 10 minutes, or until golden. Allow the muffins to cool slightly before removing to a wire rack. (The muffins may be made 1 day ahead and kept in an airtight tin.)

Lower the oven temperature to 160°C/325°F/Gas Mark 3.

Cut off the tops of the muffins and reserve. Carefully hollow out the centres of each muffin with a melon baller (reserve the crumbs for another use, such as stuffing for chicken to be roasted). Spoon some of the heated chilli into each muffin, sprinkle with chopped spring onion, replace the tops, and put on baking trays. Heat through for about 10 minutes in the oven, until the muffins and filling are warm. Serve immediately.

Individual Oysters Rockefeller

90g/3oz butter	Large dash of Pernod
225g/8oz fresh spinach,	60g/2oz dry breadcrumbs
cleaned and large stalks	30 fresh oysters, opened,
removed	drained and presented on
4 tbsp chopped fresh parsley	the half shell
4 tbsp chopped celery	60g/2oz Parmesan cheese,
1 small onion, chopped	grated
3 drops of Tabasco sauce	Seaweed (optional)
Salt and black pepper	Lemon twists, to garnish

illustrated on page 117

Makes 30

In a large saucepan, combine the butter, spinach, parsley, celery, onion, Tabasco, seasoning to taste and Pernod. Stir to combine over low heat, then cover and cook for about 15 minutes, stirring occasionally, until the spinach has wilted and the onion softened. Place the mixture in a blender or food processor, together with the breadcrumbs. Process until combined and finely chopped.

Preheat the grill to high. Position the prepared oysters on tart tins or baking dishes filled with enough rock salt to balance them. Alternatively, place the oysters in the shallow cups of bun tins. Divide the spinach mixture among the oysters, spooning a little over each one. Sprinkle a little Parmesan on top.

Grill the oysters for about 5 minutes, or until bubbling. Allow to cool slightly before arranging on a bed of seaweed, if liked, and garnishing with lemon twists.

Maine Blueberry Chewies

Maine blueberry chewies.

225g/8oz plain flour	*60g/2oz caster sugar*
Salt	*2 eggs*
2 tsp baking powder	*90g/3oz porridge oats*
1½ tsp grated nutmeg	*120g/4oz shelled walnuts,*
120g/4oz butter, softened	*chopped*
225g/8oz light brown	*120g/4oz fresh blueberries*
sugar	*Icing sugar*

illustrated on page 121

Makes about 35

Preheat the oven to 200°C/400°F/Gas mark 6. In a bowl, sift together the flour, a pinch of salt, the baking powder, cinnamon and nutmeg and mix thoroughly. In another bowl, cream the butter with the brown sugar and caster sugar until pale and fluffy. Beat in the eggs one at a time. Gradually fold in the flour mixture, together with the oats and walnuts. Stir in the berries.

Take tablespoonfuls of the batter and drop on to a greased baking sheet leaving space for them to expand. Bake in batches for about 10 minutes, or until the biscuits are golden. Remove with a fish slice and cool on wire racks. Dust with sifted icing sugar when cold. These also go well with morning coffee or as a tea-time snack.

Mexican Botanas

There is much crossover today between American Tex-Mex cooking and that of the Northern Mexican states of Sonora and Chihuahua. While seviche is a long-established Hispanic recipe, designed to preserve fish on its way inland from the coastal ports, today it is found in all the smartest restaurants from California to New York. Corn tortillas – a main constituent of tacos, nachos and numerous dishes – are a staple in US supermarkets, though other ingredients, like Mexican cheeses and many chillies, are still difficult to find outside of specialist delicatessens. The recipes here use easily obtainable items yet manage to convince with that inimitable South-of-the-border flavour.

Melon and White Cheese Sticks

450g/1 lb piece of green melon or watermelon, rind removed and cut into 2.5cm/1in cubes
350g/12oz samsoe or other chewy white cheese, cut into 2.5cm/1in cubes

1 tsp cayenne pepper
1 tsp salt
Lemon wedges, to serve

illustrated on page 123

Makes 12-14

Thread the watermelon or green melon and cheese cubes alternately on to 15-18cm/6-7in long wooden skewers (about 3 melon cubes and 2 cheese cubes to each skewer). Mix together the cayenne pepper and salt in a small bowl and sprinkle over the 'kebabs'. Pile on a serving platter and garnish with wedges of lemon to squeeze over the kebabs. This makes an attractive contrast to the Acapulco Seviche on Sticks (below).

Yucatan Sweetcorn Dip

225g/8oz bottled sweetcorn relish
3 tbsp finely chopped spring onions
½ tsp Tabasco sauce
2 canned pimientos, chopped

300ml/½ pint soured cream
60g/2oz mature Cheddar cheese, grated
Tortilla or California corn chips, to serve

Makes 450ml/¾ pint

In a saucepan, combine the sweetcorn relish, spring onions, Tabasco sauce, pimientos, soured cream and cheese. Heat gently, stirring, until well mixed and hot. Pour into a decorative bowl and serve surrounded by the tortilla or corn chips.

Salsa-Stuffed Artichoke Bottoms

2 beefsteak tomatoes, seeded and finely chopped
300g/10oz stoned black olives, finely chopped
2 canned jalapeño chillis, seeded and finely chopped
2 garlic cloves, chopped

5 tbsp finely chopped fresh coriander
3 tbsp olive oil
2 tbsp fresh lime juice
10 canned artichoke bottoms, drained

Makes 10-12

In a bowl, combine all the ingredients except the artichoke bottoms. Toss and fold to mix thoroughly. Cover and chill for 2-4 hours.

Carefull trim the bottoms of the artichokes, so that they balance easily. Toss the salsa one more time and turn into a strainer. When excess liquid has drained off, divide the salsa among the artichoke bottoms, mounding it up. Arrange the stuffed bottoms on an attractive dish and serve with the grilled meats and corn-on-the-cob.

Clockwise from the top: *melon and white cheese sticks, Acapulco seviche on sticks, poor man's fish puddings, Mexicali popcorn.*

Picadillo with Nachos

225g/8oz minced beef
225g/8oz minced pork
1 tbsp red wine vinegar
Salt and black pepper
½ tsp brown sugar
2 tbsp vegetable oil
1 onion, finely chopped
1 green pepper, seeded and
  chopped
1 garlic clove, finely
  chopped
½ tsp ground cumin

2 tbsp raisins
3 small tomatoes, seeded
  and chopped
60g/2oz stuffed green
  olives, sliced
1 tbsp tomato purée
2 tsp flaked almonds

To serve
Warmed tacos shells or
  cocktail nachos
Shredded lettuce (optional)

illustrated on page 125

**Makes about 10 tacos
or 30 nachos**

In a bowl, combine the beef, pork, vinegar, salt and pepper to taste and brown sugar. Work with the hands to mix well.

Heat the oil in a frying pan and fry the onion, green pepper and garlic for about 4 minutes or until just softened. Stir in the meat mixture, turn up the heat and cook for about 10 minutes or until the meat is browned and any liquid has evaporated. Add the remaining ingredients, except for the almonds. Cook over medium-low heat for about 15 minutes, stirring, until the mixture is dryish. (The picadillo can be made up to 3 days ahead, covered and chilled, and reheated just before serving.)

Scrape the picadillo into a decorative bowl and scatter over the almonds. Serve with the taco shells or cocktail nachos. Let the guests spoon a little of the picadillo into warmed tacos shells or on to the bite-sized nachos. If using the larger tacos shells, offer a bowl of shredded lettuce so your guests can scatter bits on top.

Poor Man's Fish Puddings

1 loaf of flat Greek bread,
  weighing about 450g/1lb
450g/1lb Emmental cheese,
  grated
4x 106g/3½ oz cans of
  'skippers' (brisling) in
  tomato sauce

1x 113g/4oz can chopped
  jalapeño peppers
1 tsp chopped fresh chives
1 tsp grated nutmeg
½ tsp cayenne pepper
1 tsp dried oregano
6 eggs
600ml/1 pint milk

illustrated on page 123

Makes about 16

Butter a long, thinnish baking dish (22 x 33cm/ 9 x 13in or 20 x 35cm/8 x 14in). Cut off the crusts of the bread and cut two layers to fit snugly in the bottom of the dish. Remove one layer and reserve; leave the other in the dish.

Sprinkle half the cheese over the bread in the dish and use half the brisling to make four rows on top, lined head to tail, marching along the length of the dish. Pour over the tomato sauce from the cans. Scatter over half the jalapeño peppers. Cover with the reserved bread slices, the remaining cheese, four more rows of brisling and the rest of the chopped peppers.

In a bowl, beat together the herbs and spices, the eggs and milk. Pour this mixture evenly over the mixture in the baking dish. Cover tightly and chill for at least 8 hours or up to 36.

Preheat the oven to 180°C/350°F/Gas Mark 4. Bake, uncovered, until the top is browned and the centre is firm to the touch, about 45 minutes. Cool for 15-20 minutes, then cut into 14-16 'fingers', each two fish deep.

Acapulco Seviche on Sticks

Picadillo with nachos.

In a large bowl, stir together the lime juice, garlic and spring onions. Drop in the halved scallops and toss gently to combine. Cover and chill for 5 hours or overnight, stirring occasionally. The scallops will become opaque.

About 1 hour before serving, drain the scallops well. Return the scallops, onion and garlic to the bowl and add the remaining ingredients except the garnish. Toss to combine well and leave for the remaining time.

Thread the scallops on to small wooden skewers, alternating with the red pepper squares. Pile on a platter and garnish with fresh coriander sprigs.

Juice of 5 limes
1 garlic clove, crushed
6 spring onions, thinly sliced
675g/1 ½ lb scallops, without corals, halved
½ tsp chilli paste
Salt and black pepper

2 tbsp finely chopped fresh coriander
1 tbsp olive oil
1 fresh green chilli, finely chopped
1 red pepper, seeded and cut into squares
Fresh coriander sprigs, to garnish

illustrated on page 123

Makes 12-14

Sopaipillas

450g/1 lb muscovado sugar

2x 7.5cm/3in cinnamon sticks

Grated zest and juice of 2 small oranges

Groundnut oil, for deep frying

Slices of orange, to decorate

Fritter dough

120g/4oz unsalted butter

60g/2oz caster sugar

Salt

150g/5oz plain flour

3 size-2 eggs

illustrated on page 127

Makes about 40

In a saucepan, combine the sugar, cinnamon sticks and orange zest. Add enough water to the orange juice to make 250ml/8fl oz and pour into the pan. Bring to the boil, stirring until the sugar is dissolved. Continue to boil for 5 minutes, then strain and allow to cool.

To make the dough, in a heavy saucepan combine 250ml/8fl oz water, the butter, sugar and salt to taste. Bring to the boil over high heat, then reduce the heat to medium, pour in the flour and beat the mixture with a wooden spoon until it leaves the sides of the pan in a ball. Remove the pan from the heat and continue beating until cool. Beat in the eggs, one at a time, to incorporate well. Allow the dough to stand for 15-20 minutes.

In a deep-fryer or heavy saucepan, heat about 5cm/2in of groundnut oil to 180°C/350°F. Drop the fritter dough in by heaped teaspoons, a few at a time. Fry, turning, for about 5 minutes or until golden and puffed, then lift out with a slotted spoon and drain on kitchen paper.

When all the fritters are cooked, arrange on a large serving platter and pour over the cooled syrup. Decorate with twists of orange and serve immediately, or chill, covered, for up to 4 hours before serving.

Sweet Potatoes with Guacamole

450g/1 lb sweet potatoes, scrubbed and ends cut off

2 tbsp sunflower oil

Salt

Soured cream, to serve

Fresh coriander sprigs, to garnish

Guacamole

Juice of ½ lime

1 tbsp finely chopped fresh coriander

1 small onion, finely chopped

2 small fresh green chillies, chopped

2 small tomatoes, seeded and chopped

Salt and black pepper

2 medium avocados

illustrated on page 127

**Makes about 30 slices
and 600ml/1 pint**

Make the guacamole: in a bowl, mix together all the guacamole ingredients except the avocados. Cover tightly and let it steep for about 3 hours. Just before making the sweet potato slices, peel and stone the avocados and cut into small pieces. Add to the rest of the guacamole ingredients. Mash and stir, thoroughly mixing, until creamy. Place the avocado stones in the guacamole until it is to be used – to keep it green – and cover.

Preheat the oven to 200°C/400°F/Gas Mark 6. Cut the potatoes into 5-6mm/¼–⅛in thick slices. Lay the slices in a single layer on greased baking tray(s), brush with the oil and sprinkle with salt. Bake for about 25 minutes, turning once and redistributing the slices to brown evenly.

Transfer the slices in a single layer to a serving platter. Spoon some of the guacamole on to each slice and top with a small dollop of soured cream. Serve warm or at room temperature, garnished with coriander sprigs.

Left: *sweet potatoes with guacamole.* Right: *sopaipillas.*

Mexicali Popcorn

4 heaped tbs unpopped
  popcorn
90g/3oz shelled pistachio
  nuts
225g/8oz light brown
  sugar
Salt

120ml/4fl oz golden syrup
60g/2oz butter
1 tsp ground cinnamon
½ tsp grated nutmeg
4 tbsp whipping cream
1 tsp vanilla essence

illustrated on page 123

Makes about 1.8 litres/3 pints

Preheat the oven to low.

Pop the popcorn in a popper, or in a heavy, closed saucepan with a little oil. When all has popped, turn the popcorn into a greased baking tray. Add the pistachios and place in the oven to keep warm.

In a large heavy saucepan, combine the sugar, salt to taste, golden syrup, butter, cinnamon, nutmeg and cream. Stir over medium heat until the sugar dissolves and the mixture is creamy. Then stop stirring and let the mixture boil gently until it reaches 138°C/280°F on a sugar thermometer. Remove from the heat and thoroughly stir in the vanilla essence.

Take the baking tray from the oven and immediately pour the toffee over the popcorn and nuts. Stir gently to coat and allow the mixture to cool. When it is no longer sticky, break up into small pieces. (This can be served immediately or stored in an airtight container for several days.)

Barbequed Bites

Menu

Classic American Barbecue Burgers

Prawns in Bacon

Glazed Ribs

Garlic Vegetables on a Stick

Grilled Herbed Corn

Percan Pie Squares

Clockwise from the top: *leek and carrot sticks, individual smoked salmon roulades, Gruyère and smoked salmon popovers, steak Tartare balls with mustard sauce, strawberry tartlets.*

Classic American Barbecue Burgers

900g/2 lb lean minced beef	**To serve**
1 size-2 egg	*8 toasted sesame bread rolls*
Salt and Black pepper	*or baps, split open*
120ml/4fl oz treacle or	*1 large onion, cut into*
molasses	*rings*
4 tbsp Dijon mustard	*3 large gherkins, sliced*
1 tsp garlic paste	*lengthways*
1 tbsp soy sauce	*2 tomatoes, sliced*
4 tbsp red wine vinegar	*Lettuce wedges*
2 tbsp mild chilli sauce	*Mayonnaise*
4 tbsp tomato ketchup	

illustrated on page 129

Makes 8

In a large bowl, work the meat with your hands. Add the egg and salt and pepper to taste, and continue to work until combined. Divide into 8 equal portions and shape each into a flattened cake or patty. Cover and chilled until needed.

In another bowl, mix together the treacle or molasses, mustard, garlic paste, soy sauce, vinegar, chilli sauce and ketchup. Combine well.

When the barbeque coals are ashen, place the patties on the grill and baste liberally with the sauce. Cook, basting and turning once or twice, until the patties are done as preferred – about 5 minutes for rare, 12 for well done.

Serve the hamburgers from the grill, using a fish slice to turn them into the split rolls. Let guests help themselves from a generous platter of garnishes: onion, sliced gherkins, tomatoes, lettuce, and mayonnaise, tomato ketchup and mustard or hand them round already garnished.

Prawns in Bacon

120ml/4fl oz olive oil	*raw prawns, shelled and*
2 tbsp white wine vinegar	*deveined, tails*
3 garlic cloves, crushed	*intact*
2 tbsp finely chopped fresh	*7-8 rashers of rindless*
oregano	*streaky bacon, cut in half*
450g/1 lb large headless	*lengthways*

illustrated on page 128

Makes about 14

In a large bowl, combine the oil, vinegar, garlic and oregano, mixing well. Add the prawns and toss to coat. Cover and chill for at least 8 hours or overnight in the refrigerator.

Drain the prawns and wrap each in a piece of bacon, securing with a wooden cocktail stick. When the coals of the barbecue are ashen and very hot (after about 35 minutes), lay the prawns on the grill and barbecue for about 10 minutes, turning once, until they are opaque. Watch to be sure that the prawns don't burn or the bacon crisp. If they flame too much, use a water sprayer to dampen down the fire a little.

These prawns go particularly well with the garlic vegetables on a stick.

Glazed Ribs

1 garlic clove, crushed	*1 tbsp cider vinegar*
1 tbsp olive oil	*1 tbsp grated orange zest*
1 tbsp Worcestershire sauce	*1.4kg/3lb pork spare ribs,*
Salt and black pepper	*trimmed into separate ribs*
175g/6fl oz redcurrant jelly	
Large pinch of cayenne	**To garnish**
pepper	*Orange twists*
1 tsp brown sugar	*Watercress sprigs*

illustrated on page 128

Makes about 20-25

In a large saucepan, combine the garlic and oil over medium heat and cook until the garlic is softened. Stir in the Worcestershire sauce, seasoning to taste, redcurrant jelly, cayenne pepper, brown sugar, cider vinegar and grated orange zest. Bring to the boil and boil for 1 minute, then remove from the heat. (This can be made up to 2 days ahead and kept, covered and chilled.)

Preheat the oven to 180°C/350°F/Gas Mark 4. Brush both sides of the ribs with the sauce and bake in the oven for about 1 hour. Remove and reserve until the coals of the barbecue are ready.

When the coals are ashen and very hot, lay the ribs on the grill and brush with more of the sauce. Cook and turn, basting occasionally, for about 20-30 minutes, until the ribs are browned and tender. Arrange on a platter garnished with orange twists and watercress sprigs.

Garlic Vegetables on a Stick

1 red pepper, cored, seeded and cut into 5cm/2in strips
1 yellow pepper, cored, seeded and cut into 5cm/2in strips
350g/12oz button mushrooms
3 medium courgettes, cut into 2.5cm/1in diagonal chunks
12 shallots, halved

2 small bulbs of fennel, trimmed and sliced vertically
Fresh mint leaves, to garnish

Garlic oil
120ml/4fl oz olive oil
2 garlic cloves, crushed
Pinch of cayenne pepper
Salt and black pepper

illustrated on page 129

Makes about 12

Make the garlic oil: in a saucepan combine the oil, garlic, cayenne pepper and seasoning to taste. Cook over a low heat until hot but not boiling. Remove from the heat and allow to cool. (The oil will keep, bottled, in a cool, dark place for about 1 week.)

Thread the vegetables on to 15cm/6in skewers, mixing them attractively. When the barbecue coals are ashen, lay the skewers (in batches, if necessary) on the grill and brush liberally with the garlic oil. Cook, turning, for about 10 minutes, until the vegetables are browned and softened. Continue to brush with the oil during cooking.

Take the skewers off the grill and arrange on a platter, garnished with fresh mint leaves.

Grilled Herbed Corn-on-the-Cob

120g/4oz butter, softened
2 tbsp finely chopped fresh sage

8 ears of corn-on-the-cob, husked
Lemon salt or herb seasoning, to serve

illustrated on page 129

Serves 8

In a bowl, blend the butter and fresh sage, mashing and stirring to combine well. (The butter mixture can be made ahead and formed into a log. It will keep, covered and chilled, for up to 3 days..)

When ready to cook the sweetcorn, soften a little of the butter and spread it all over the corn-on-the-cob. Wrap each separately in heavy-duty foil. Cut the remaining butter into pieces for serving.

When the coals are ashen, place the wrapped corn on the grill. Bake for 15-20 minutes, turning several times. Serve with the sage butter and the lemon salt or herb seasoning to sprinkle on to taste.

Pecan Pie Squares

150g/5oz plain flour
90g/3oz porridge oats
175g/6oz soft light brown sugar
120g/4oz butter, softened

Filling
3 eggs
4 tbsp treacle

120ml/4fl oz golden syrup
90g/3oz shelled pecan nuts, chopped
1 tbsp plain flour
Salt
½ tsp rum flavouring

To decorate
Whipped cream
Pecan nut halves

illustrated on page 128

Makes 26-30

Preheat the oven to 180°C/350°F/Gas Mark 4. In a bowl, combine the flour, oats and brown sugar; mix well. Rub in the butter with the fingertips until the mixture resembles breadcrumbs. Press over the bottom of a 20 or 23cm/8 or 9 inch square cake tin. Bake the pastry base for about 15 minutes, until slightly coloured.

Meanwhile, in a bowl, beat together all the filling ingredients until well combined. Pour the filling over the pastry base and bake for about 30 minutes longer.

Cool in the tin on a wire rack, then cut into squares. (These can be frozen for future use.)

Before serving, pipe rosettes of whipped cream on to each square, and top with a pecan half.

131

Raise Your Glasses

Toast the hosts – who can provide a selection of drinks as varied and flavourful as the food. It is not unusual to expend all our energy on planning and preparing edibles, only to relax when it comes to liquid refreshment. The old standbys – wine, beer, mineral water and juices – can seem so unimaginative when a real lift could only be provided by something completely different. A hot toddy at a chilly winter gathering; a spirited but balanced punch on a summer's afternoon; a traditional wine cup or a never-guess non-alcoholic blend, can all make the party go with a swing.

SPIRIT-FREE THIRST QUENCHERS

Old-Fashioned Spiced Lemonade

Serves about 15

500ml/16fl oz fresh lemon juice
450g/1 lb caster sugar
15 cloves
5 cinnamon sticks, each 5cm/2in long
Thinly sliced lemons

Strain the lemon juice into a jug. In a large saucepan, dissolve the sugar in 450ml/¾ pint water over high heat, stirring; bring to the boil. Add the cloves and cinnamon and continue to simmer for about 6 minutes. Take off the heat and pour the lemon juice into the saucepan. Allow to cool, then chill for several hours or overnight, covered.

Just before serving, dilute the syrup with 2.4 litres/4 pints iced water in a large punchbowl, or divide between 2 large jugs. Serve in glasses garnished with lemon slices.

Sunshine Orangeade

Serves 8

225g/8oz caster sugar
4 tbsp freshly grated orange zest
1.2 litres/2 pints fresh orange juice
Ice cubes
1½ bottles of soda water (1 litre/1¾ pints)
Thin orange wedges

In a saucepan, combine the sugar and the orange zest. Pour over 500ml/16fl oz water and bring to the boil, stirring. Simmer until the sugar has dissolved, then lower the heat and simmer for a further 10-12 minutes. Take off the heat and let the syrup cool. Strain the syrup, pressing on the zest to extract the juices. cover and chill. (This syrup will keep for several weeks, covered and chilled.)

In a large jug, stir together the orange syrup and the orange juice. Add the ice cubes as desired, and fill the jug with the soda water. Garnish the orangeade with the thinly sliced orange wedges and serve immediately. (Children love this!)

Classic Lemon Barley Water

Serves about 20

6 plump lemons
120g/4oz pearl barley, rinsed and drained
120g/4oz caster sugar
Lemon zest twists

Pare the zest from the lemons, taking no pith with the zest. Place the zest in a small saucepan and pour over just enough water to cover. Bring to the boil, then turn down the heat and simmer for about 5 minutes. Take off the heat and allow to cool slightly, then divide the mixture between two 2 litre/3½ pint jugs and keep cool.

Place the barley in a large saucepan and cover with water. Bring to the boil and cook for a few minutes. Drain the barley, return to the pan, cover with fresh water, agitate to rinse and drain again. Divide the drained barley between the two jugs.

Peel any remaining pith off the lemons. Cut the flesh into small pieces and divide the pieces between the jugs. Place the sugar in a small saucepan and cover with 250ml/8fl oz water. Bring to the boil and cook until syrupy. Pour over the lemon mixtures in the two jugs.

Bring another 3.5 litres/6 pints water to the boil and pour into the two jugs. Chill, covered, overnight. Strain and place in a large punchbowl or return to the two cleaned jugs. Garnish with the lemon zest twists. (Alternatively, strain into bottles and keep, chilled, for up to 1 week. This can be used as a base for punches or simple mixed soft drinks, using grenadine syrup etc.)

From left to right: *Sunshine Orangeade, Lemon Barley and Old Fashioned Lemonade*

Sparkling Virgin Marys

Serves 16

1 litre/1¾ pints tomato juice, chilled
2 tsp Tabasco sauce
4 tbsp fresh lime juice
Celery salt
1 litre/1¾ pints sparkling mineral water
Ice cubes
32 pickled cocktail onions
2 limes, each cut into 8 wedges

Divide the tomato juice, Tabasco sauce, lime juice and celery salt to taste between two jugs. Stir in the sparkling mineral water and ice cubes, as desired.

Take a cocktail stick and thread on two cocktail onions and a lime wedge. Place in a glass, and repeat with the remaining onions and lime wedges. Pour the Virgin Marys into the garnished glasses and serve.

From left to right: *Tropical Blush, Sparkling Virgin Marys, Exotic Fruit Flips (jug and glass); Watermelon Slush and Gingered Apple Zinger.*

Watermelon Slush

Serves about 8

900g/2 lb watermelon, peeled, seeded and cubed
350ml/12fl oz unsweetened apple juice
120ml/4fl oz fresh lime juice
300g/10oz caster sugar
2 egg whites
Lime slices

In the bowl of a food processor with a metal blade, combine half the watermelon cubes, the apple juice, lime juice and 150-175g/5-6oz sugar. Process until smooth; add the remaining watermelon and continue to process until smoothly slushy. Chill.

Whisk the egg whites until just frothy. Pour the rest of the sugar onto a large plate. Dip the rims of tall glasses in the egg white and then in the sugar. Divide the watermelon mixture between the glasses, garnish with lime slices and serve immediately.

Tropical Blush

Serves 12

600ml/1 pint unsweetened pineapple juice, chilled
1 (75cl) bottle or can of white grape juice
175ml/6fl oz grenadine syrup
2 bottles of sparkling mineral water
  (750ml/1¼ pints each)
Ice cubes
12 maraschino cherries
12 pineapple slices, fresh or canned

Pour the juices and the grenadine syrup into a large punchbowl. Stir vigorously to combine. Pour in the mineral water and add ice cubes, as desired.

Spear 12 cocktail sticks with a cherry and a pineapple slice. Distribute among 12 glasses and ladle the punch into them.

Exotic Fruit Flips

Serves about 15

1 medium Charentais melon, peeled, seeded and cubed
5 ripe passion fruit, pulped
1 ripe mango, peeled, seeded and cubed
250ml/8fl oz fresh mandarin or ruby orange juice
1 litre/1¾ pints ginger ale or Seven-Up
Ice cubes

In the bowl of a food processor with a metal blade, combine the melon flesh, passion fruit pulp, mango flesh and a little of the mandarin juice and process until smooth. Pour the purée into a large jug or divide between two smaller jugs; add the remaining mandarin juice and the ginger ale. Add ice cubes, as desired, and serve immediately in champagne or tall wine glasses.

Gingered Apple Zinger

Serves about 8

500ml/16fl oz unsweetened apple juice
120g/4oz stem ginger in syrup
12 cinnamon sticks, each 5cm/2in long
1½ bottles of sparkling mineral water
  (1 litre/1¾ pints each)
2 apples, cored and cut into eighths
Ice cubes

In a large saucepan, mix together the apple juice, ginger and its syrup and the cinnamon. Bring to the boil, then lower the heat and simmer until the liquid is reduced by about half. Stir occasionally to prevent burning. Remove from the heat and allow to cool. Chill overnight.

Pour the liquid into a punchbowl. Pour over the mineral water and stir in the apple slices and ice cubes. Serve in punch glasses.

HOT DRINKS AND PUNCHES

The Bishop

Serves about 30

5 (75cl) bottles of Beaujolais
1 cinnamon stick
8 cloves
1 tsp grated nutmeg
2 tsp ground mixed spice
Thinly pared zest of orange, cut into shreds
225g/8oz sugar
½ (75cl) bottle of medium-dry sherry
200ml/7fl oz brandy

Pour the wine into a large saucepan or flameproof casserole. Add the spices, orange zest and sugar and heat slowly, about 20 minutes, stirring to gradually dissolve the sugar. Never let the punch boil during the heating.

Pour in the sherry and continue stirring over a low heat for another 15 minutes. Add more sugar or spices to taste. Stir in the brandy and heat for another 10 minutes. Take off the heat and serve in mugs or in heatproof glasses.

Hot Buttered Rum

Serves about 12

12 sugar lumps
1 (75cl) bottle of golden rum
90g/3oz unsalted butter
Grated nutmeg

Place a lump of sugar in the bottom of each of 12 warmed or heatproof whisky glasses. Fill two-thirds full with hot water, add 4 tablespoons of rum to each glass, and top with a small slice of butter. Sprinkle with nutmeg and serve immediately.

Tom & Jerry

Serves 12

12 eggs, separated
4 heaped tbsp caster sugar
1½ tsp bicarbonate of soda
275ml/9fl oz brandy
175ml/6fl oz rum
1.2 litres/2 pints hot milk
Grated nutmeg

In a large bowl, whisk the egg whites until frothy. Whisk in the sugar, 1 tablespoon at a time, and continue whisking until the whites stand in stiff peaks. In a large punch bowl, beat the egg yolks until they are thick and lemon-coloured. Fold the whites into the yolks, sprinkling over the bicarbonate of soda.

Gently whisk in the brandy, then the rum. Pour in the hot milk, whisking. Serve immediately in mugs, dusting a little nutmeg over each serving.

Viennese Glühwein

Serves about 25

4 (75cl) bottles of dry red wine
350g/12oz soft light brown sugar
3 lemons, each stuck with 5 cloves
8 cinnamon sticks, each 5cm/2in long
1 (75cl) bottle of brandy

From left to right: *Yuletide Log, New English Mulled Cider, Viennese Glühwein, Tom & Jerry and The Bishop*

Pour the wine into a large saucepan or flameproof casserole and add the sugar and clove studded lemons. Simmer gently for about 5 minutes, stirring to dissolve the sugar. Remove from the heat and stir in the brandy. Ladle the glühwein into warmed or heatproof glasses.

Yuletide Glögg

Serves about 12

1 (75cl) bottle of aquavit
2 (75cl) bottles of red Côtes du Rhone
120g/4oz sugar
90g/3oz sultanas
1 tbsp Cardamon seeds
7 cloves
5cm/2in cinnamon stick
½ tsp grated lemon zest
12 slices of lemon

Pour half the aquavit and all the wine into a large saucepan or flameproof casserole. Stir in the sugar and sultanas. Tie the spices and lemon zest in a muslin bag and drop it into the glögg. Heat slowly and bring just to the boil, then cover and simmer for about 10 minutes.

Pour in the remaining aquavit and remove from the heat. Remove the spice bag, then set the top of the punch alight. Serve immediately in heatproof glasses, floating a lemon slice in each glass.

New England Mulled Cider

Serves about 20

4 litres/7 pints dry cider
300ml/½ pint Triple Sec, orange Curaçao or Cointreau
120g/4oz raisins
2 oranges, unpeeled, sliced
1 apple, quartered, cored and sliced
2 lemons, unpeeled, sliced
120g/4oz soft light brown sugar
10 pieces star anise
2 tsp grated nutmeg
2 cinnamon sticks
2 tsp ground allspice
14 cloves
250ml/8fl oz dark rum

In a large saucepan or flameproof casserole, combine all the ingredients except the rum. Heat over medium heat, but do not allow to boil, for about 15 minutes. Just before serving, stir in the rum. Serve hot in mugs.

WINE AND CHAMPAGNE COOLERS

Spanish Sangria

Serves about 12

2 (75cl) bottles of red Rioja, chilled
1 litre/1¾ pints soda water or sparkling mineral water, chilled
2 tsp caster sugar
Large pinch of ground cinnamon
Lemon slices
Orange slices
Ice cubes (optional)

In a large punchbowl, combine the Rioja and soda water. In a cup, dissolve the sugar in 1-2 tablespoons warm water and stir the solution into the wine, together with cinnamon to taste. Add lemon and orange slices, and ice cubes if desired. Stir to combine thoroughly.

Strawberry Delight Punch

Serves about 20

700g/1½ lb strawberries
1 litre/2 pints strawberry sorbet
250ml/8fl oz unsweetened grapefruit juice
2.4 litres/4 pints guava-passion fruit drink
1 (75cl) bottle of sparkling white wine

Reserve about half the strawberries, choosing the prettiest, and keep the hulls attached. Place them on a tray and freeze until hard, about 1 hour. Then package in a freezer bag until needed.

Scoop the sorbet into small balls, place on a tray and freeze for about 1 hour. Then remove to a plastic container and freeze until needed. (Don't keep the frozen fruit or sorbet balls longer than about 2 days before using.)

Hull the remaining berries and place in the bowl of a food processor, together with the grapefruit juice. Process until puréed.

In a large glass punchbowl, combine the purée, the guava-passion fruit drink and the wine. Stir to mix well. Add the sorbet balls, and float the frozen strawberries on top. Serve in whisky or other wide-mouthed glasses, with spoons.

From left to right: *Pink Shocker, Louisiana Mint Cooler, Henley Special, Planters Wine Punch and Strawberry Delight Punch*

Louisiana Mint Cooler

Serves about 20

2 tbsp Indian tea leaves
2 tbsp chopped fresh mint
3 (75cl) bottles of claret
120ml/4fl oz fresh lemon juice
250ml/8fl oz honey
1 litre/1¾ pints sparkling mineral water
Lemon slices
Fresh mint sprigs
Ice cubes

Pour 1 litre/1¾ pints of boiling water over the tea leaves and mint. Leave to steep for about 5 minutes, then strain the mint tea into a large punchbowl. Leave to cool thoroughly.

Pour in the wine, lemon juice, honey and sparkling water. Stir to combine, and garnish with lemon slices prepared with mint leaves. Add ice cubes as desired.

Planter's Wine Punch

Serves 20

2 (75cl) bottles of dry white wine
900ml/1½ pints unsweetened pineapple juice
700g/1½ lb strawberries, hulled and thinly sliced
4 kiwi fruit, peeled and sliced
6 tbsp brandy

In a large glass punchbowl, mix together the wine and pineapple juice. Add the sliced fruit to the punch and stir in the brandy. Finally, add two or three trays of ice cubes to the punch, stir well and serve immediately. A real thirst quencher.

Henley Special

Serves about 25

225g/8oz strawberries, hulled and halved
2 small peaches or nectarines, peeled, stoned and sliced
120g/4oz small seedless grapes
120g/4oz caster sugar
175ml/6fl oz kirsch
½ (75cl) bottle of sweet white vermouth
5 (75cl) bottles of fruity white wine
1 (75cl) bottle of sparkling white wine, chilled

In a large punchbowl, combine the fruit, sugar and kirsch; toss to mix well. Leave for 2 hours.

Pour over the vermouth and carefully stir into the fruit. Add the wine and stir to combine. Just before serving pour over the sparkling wine.

Serve the punch in decorative glasses.

Pink Shocker

Serves about 25

2 (75cl) bottles of dry rosé wine, chilled
Juice of 4 lemons, chilled
1 tsp caster sugar
900ml/1½ pints raspberry sorbet, slightly softened
1 (75cl) bottle of pink Champagne or pink sparkling wine
Ice cubes

Pour the rose wine into a large punchbowl. In a small bowl, combine the lemon juice and caster sugar, stirring until dissolved. Add the sugared juice to the rosé wine, scoop in the sorbet, and pour over the champagne. Add the ice cubes and serve immediately.

SPIRITED ENTERTAINERS

Old-Fashioned Eggnog

Serves about 25

12 eggs, separated
225g/8oz caster sugar
600ml/1 pint milk
250ml/8fl oz dark rum
500ml/16fl oz bourbon whisky
600ml/1 pint double cream
1 tsp vanilla essence
Freshly grated nutmeg
Ground cinnamon

In a large punchbowl, beat the egg yolks, then add the sugar and continue beating until smooth and lemon-coloured. Add the milk, rum and bourbon whisky. In a large mixing bowl, whisk 9 of the egg whites until they hold stiff peaks, and in another bowl whip the double cream until thick. Stir the vanilla essence into the egg yolk mixture, then fold in the whisked egg whites and the whipped cream, mixing gently but thoroughly. Cover and chill for about 4 hours.

Just before serving, whisk the remaining 3 egg whites until stiff and fold them gently into the eggnog. Sprinkle with nutmeg and cinnamon and serve immediately.

Pitcher Moscow Mules

Serves 12

Ice cubes
550ml/18fl oz vodka
350ml/12fl oz lemon juice
10 cans of ginger beer (325ml/11fl oz each), chilled

Turn the contents of two ice cube trays into each of two large jugs. Divide the vodka, lemon juice and ginger beer between the jugs, stir well and serve immediately in tall glasses.

Caribbean Spritzer Punch

Serves 12-15

1 litre/ 1¾ pints unsweetened pineapple juice
550ml/18fl oz light rum
250ml/8fl oz bottled lime juice
2 bottles of soda water or sparkling mineral water
 (1 litre/1¾ pints each)
Ice cubes
1 small Charentais melon, cut into small slices

In a punchbowl, combine the unsweetened pineapple juice, rum and lime juice. Pour in the soda and add ice cubes as desired. Ladle into glasses and garnish with the melon slices.

Pitcher Piña Coladas

Serves about 10

450ml/¾ pint light rum
300ml/½ pint canned cream of coconut, or 150g/5oz
 block creamed coconut mixed with 150ml/¼ pint
 hot water
750ml/1¼ pints unsweetened pineapple juice
2.4 litres/ 4 pints ice cubes
20 small wedges of fresh pineapple
Maraschino cherries

In the bowl of a food processor with a metal blade, combine the rum, cream of coconut, pineapple juice and ice cubes, and process until smooth. (Do this in batches, if necessary.) Divide the mixture between two large, chilled glass jugs and serve immediately in glasses garnished with the pineapple wedges and the Maraschino cherries.

Mint Juleps

Serves about 12

12 sugar lumps
Crushed ice
1½ (70cl) bottles of bourbon whisky
Fresh mint sprigs

Mint juleps are traditionally presented in silver mugs or goblets, but glasses will do. In a bowl, dissolve the 12 sugar lumps in 600ml/1 pint hot water. Stir to make the syrup.

Fill each mug or glass with crushed ice, and pour over bourbon whisky until the ice is almost covered. Stir the ice and whisky in each mug until the outside is frosted and some of the ice has melted. Stir in sugar syrup to taste. Fill a side of each mug generously with fresh mint sprigs, and serve immediately before the ice melts too much.

Mexican Spitfire

Serves 12

550ml/18fl oz tequila
350ml/12fl oz bottled lime juice
350ml/12fl oz Triple Sec or orange Curaçao
1 fresh red or green chilli, seeded and thinly sliced
2 bottles of soda water or sparkling mineral water
 (1 litre/ 1¾ pints), chilled
Ice cubes
Salt
12 lime slices

Divide the tequila, lime juice and Triple Sec between 2 large jugs and add half the chilli slices to each. Chill for 4-5 hours. Just before serving, divide the soda between them and add as many ice cubes as desired. Stir to combine. Serve in glasses whose rims have been dipped in iced water and then coated in coarse sea salt and garnished with a lime slice.

From left to right: *Mexican Spitfire, Pina Colada, Moscow Mule, Old Fashioned Egg Nog & Caribbean Punch*

Index

A

Aïoli 71
Albondigas 40
Almonds
  Cantonese, biscuits 78
  Valencian 41
Alsatian cocktail balls 70
Apricot
  and raspberry tartlets 51
  nutty mounds 82
Artichokes
  feta filled 22
  and prawn cups 34
  salsa-stuffed 122
  and tomato barquettes 22
Aubergine sambal 89
Avocado
  and carrot squares 98
  and scrambled eggs 52
  with Aruba salt cod cakes 109

B

Banana
  deep fried kebabs 108
  lime tarts 104
Beef
  and smoked ham cigars 99
  Caribbean jerky 106
Beef (mince)
  Burgers, classic American 130
  chilli 120
  and coconut, peanut grills 108
  dumplings 102
  easy kebbeh 24
  fancy Swedish meatballs 56
  finger cabbage rolls 28
  picadillo 124
  steak tartare balls 35
  Teriyaki beef cakes 45
Beetroot, stuffed baby 26
Blueberry chewies 121
Bread pudding 60
Broccoli fritters 86
Brussels sprouts, chestnut stuffed 60
Biscuits
  Cantonese almond 78
  Cheddar-hazelnut crackers 62
  cheese and mango 111
  Florentines 70

  fruitcake 51
Burgers, classic American 130

C

Cabbage, finger rolls 28
Cakes
  cinnamon spirals 50
  doughnuts 115
  lemon squares 99
  Maine blueberry chewies 121
  Nevis fruit bakes 111
  peanut butter and chocolate bars 115
  pecan pie squares 131
  scones, sweet potato cheese 50
Caponata, filled tomatoes 92
Carrot and leek sticks 34
Caviar, with new potatoes 26
Celery, with pesto 90
Char chiu buns 76
Cheese
  Cheddar-hazelnut crackers 62
  and mango biscuits 111
  Croque-Monsieurs 72
  curd cheese and ham piroshki 30
  dates, with cheese stuffing 82
  feta filled artichokes 22
  Gruyère and smoked ham popovers 34
  melon and white cheese sticks 122
  scones 50
  Stilton-walnut grapes 61
Chestnut stuffed Brussels 60
Chicken
  Creole wings 98
  hot sweet and sour drum sticks 77
  and lamb sate 100
  mango Waldorf sandwiches 50
  spiced samosas 86
  Yakitori 42
Chilli, with muffins 120
Chinese leaves, with spicy meat 74
Choux buns 82
Cider, New England mulled 137
Cinnamon spirals 50
Coriander dip 86

Courgettes
  garlic curls 68
  Goanese stuffed 84
  and lentil patties 24
Crab
  Jamaican dip 110
  and prawn palmiers 83
Cranberry relish 57
Croque-Monsieurs 72
Crostini 95
Cruditees with aioli 71
Cucumber
  minted sandwiches 51
  and prawn bowls 98

D

Dates, with cheese stuffing 82
Devils on horseback 83
Dips
  coriander 86
  garlic 40
  Jamaican crab 110
  mango 102
  roasted pepper 40
  spicy peanut 116
  spinach 94
  tomato 118
  Yucatan sweetcorn 122
Doughnuts, potato 115

E

Eggnog, old fashioned 140
Eggs
  and bacon bundles 108
  creamy in bread cases 88
  with devilled ham 67
  miniature Scotch 62
  orange 56
  scrambled egg avocados 52
  tarragon cream 68
  tonnato stuffed 93
Empanadas, vegetable 38

F

Fish (see also prawns, crab, tuna, squid, smoked)
  Aruba salt cod cakes 109
  miniature fish cakes 44
  poor man's fish puddings 124
Florentines, black and white 70

Frankfurter boats 114
Fruit
  and cinnamon dipping sauce 79

  chocolate dipped 99
Fruitcake biscuits 51

G

Garlic dip 40
Ginger roll 46
Gluhwien, Viennese 136
Grapes, Stilton-walnut 61
Gravadlax, sandwiches 54
Guacamole 126

H

Ham
  and beef cigars 99
  and curd cheese piroshki 30
  Croque-Monsieurs 72
  devilled, in eggs 67
  and Gruyère popovers 34
Herring and apple rolls 31
Hummus 20

J

Jerky, Caribbean 106

K

Kabanos and papaya sticks 83
Kebbeh, easy 24

L

Lamb
  and almond kebabs 87
  and chicken saté 100
  cider-baked cutlets 63
  miniature shish kebabs 25
Lamb (mince)
  stuffed vine leaves 20
Leek and carrot sticks 34
Lemon
  barley water, classic 132
  cheese, pancakes 55
  curd, fruit-topped tartlets 88
  sauce 45, 108
  squares 99

Lemonade, old fashioned
    spiced 132
Lentil and courgette patties
    24
Lychee-pineapple bites 105

M

Mango dip 102
Meatballs
    Albondigas 40
    Swedish 56
Melon
    baskets 66
    and white cheese sticks 122
Mint julep 141
Muffins
    pineapple with pork 110
    Southwestern corn 120
Mushrooms
    marinated 29
    on toast 66
    spicy stuffed 72
Mussels, stuffed Casino 39
Mustard sauce 35, 58

N

Nevis fruit bakes 111
Nibbles
    buttered Brazil chips 106
    fuselli crunchies 94
    Mexicali popcorn 127
    spiced pistachio brittle 82
    split and chick pea nibbles
    84
    sunshine mix 103
    sweet fried nuts 74
    toasted pumpkin seeds 47

O

Olives
    fennel scented 73
    Italian market 90
    tapenade toasts 70
Orangeade 132
Oysters
    open faced sandwiches 58
    Rockefeller 120

P

Pancakes, lemon cheese 55
Papaya and kabanos sticks 83
Peaches, hash stuffed 83
Peanut
    butter and chocolate bars
    115
    sauce 100
    spicy spread 116
Pecan pie squares 131

Peppers
    roasted, dip 40
    with savoury filling 40
Pesto 90
Phyllo pastry 22, 72
Picadillo, with nachos 124
Pina colada 140
Pineapple
    lychee bites 105
    muffins 110
Piroshki 30
Pizzas, quick child-size 114
Polenta, puffs 94
Popcorn, Mexicali 127
Pork
    char chiu buns 76
    glazed ribs 130
    Jamaican 110
Pork (mince)
    albondigas 40
    fancy Swedish meatballs 56
    picadillo 124
    potato croquettes with
    surprise filling 28
    spicy meat in Chinese leaves
    74
    spring rolls 42
Potatoes
    croquettes with surprise
    filling 28
    new with caviar 26
    piggy back 115
    skins with sour cream 119
    sweet, crisps 110
    sweet and sour 52
    sweet with guacamole 126
Prawns
    and artichoke cups 34
    and crab palmiers 83
    crackers 100
    and cucumber bowls 98
    deep fried 36
    in bacon 130
    toasts 78
    vol-au-vents 56
Prunes
    devils on horseback 83
    surprises 72
Punches
    Caribbean spritzer 140
    planter's wine 139
    strawberry delight 138

Q

Quails' eggs, poached in
    tomatoes 67

R

Redcurrant sauce 56
Rice croquettes 76
Rum, hot buttered 136

S

Salad
    citrus mixed lettuce cup 116
    Costa Blanca boats 36
Salmon tartlets 30
Salsa 122
Samosas, spiced chicken 86
Sandwiches
    biscuit cutter 114
    mango Waldorf chicken 50
    miniature Reuben 118
    minted cucumber 51
    open-faced gravadlax 54
    open-faced oyster 58
Sangria, Spanish 138
Sardines
    lemon-onion 38
    Sicilian paste 95
Saté, lamb and chicken 100
Sauces
    dipping 24, 25, 47, 76, 86
    lemon 45, 108
    mustard 35, 58
    peanut 100
    redcurrant 56
    tartare 54
Sauerkrout
    Alsatian cocktail balls 70
    Reuben sandwiches 118
Sausages
    baby bangers `n' mash 67
    rolls 60
Scallops
    Acapulco seviche on sticks
    125
    raddichio and goat cheese
    bites 92
Scones, sweet potato cheese
    50
Scotch eggs, miniature 62
Smoked salmon roulades 34
Smoked haddock croquettes
    54
Smoked trout mousse 82
Sopaipillas 126
Spring rolls 42
Spinach
    dip 94
    phyllo triangles 22
Squid, stuffed 102
Steak Tartare balls 35
Strawberry
    delight punch 138
    tartlets 35
Sushi, grilled tuna 44
Sweetcorn
    grilled on-the-cob 131
    mini 'oysters' 66
    spiced baby 103
    Yucatan dip 122
Sweet dishes
    banana lime tarts 104
    chocolate dipped fruit 99
    deep fried banana kebabs
    108

East-West ginger roll 46
fruit-topped lemon curd
    tartlets 88
fruit with cinnamon dipping
    sauce 79
lemon cheese pancakes 55
lychee-pineapple bites 105
melon baskets 66
sopaipillas 126
strawberry tartlets 35
whisky-scented bread
    pudding 60

T

Tabbouleh 98
Tapenade 70
Tartare sauce 54
Tartlets
    apricot and raspberry 51
    artichoke and tomato
    barquettes 22
    banana lime 104
    dilled salmon 30
    fruit-topped lemon curd 88
    strawberry 35
Tomatoes
    and artichoke barquettes 22
    caponata-filled 92
    dip 118
    with poached quails' eggs 67
Tortellini, garlicky mixed 93
Tuna
    grilled sushi 44
    stuffed eggs 93
Turkey puffs 57

V

Vegetables
    balls 118
    Empanadas 38
    lettuce rolls 104
    on a stick 131
    pickled baby 46
Vine leaves, stuffed 20

W

Watermelon
    candied 88
    slush 134

Y

Yakitori chicken 42

Acknowledgements

Editorial – Norma Macmillan, Harriet Ashworth,
Cheryl Jacob, Lucinda Tam
Photography – Don Wood
Home economists – Jill Eggleton, Hilary Foster
Stylist – Carolyn Russell
Design – Ran Barnes and Roger Abraham at The Creative Space
Illustrations – Paul Bailey
Administration – Jenny Sutcliffe
Production – Peter Price
Publisher – Nigel Perryman